DATE DUE

DEC 8 '99			

DEMCO 38-296

Realism in nineteenth-century music

Realism in nineteenth-century music

CARL DAHLHAUS

PROFESSOR OF MUSIC HISTORY
TECHNISCHE UNIVERSITÄT, W. BERLIN

TRANSLATED BY

MARY WHITTALL

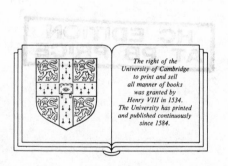

The right of the
University of Cambridge
to print and sell
all manner of books
was granted by
Henry VIII in 1534.
The University has printed
and published continuously
since 1584.

CAMBRIDGE UNIVERSITY PRESS

CAMBRIDGE

LONDON   NEW YORK   NEW ROCHELLE
MELBOURNE   SYDNEY

the University of Cambridge
Street, Cambridge CB2 1RP
ork, NY 10022, USA
Melbourne 3166, Australia

Originally published in German as
Musikalischer Realismus: Zur Musikgeschichte des 19. Jahrhunderts
by R. Piper & Co. Verlag, Munich 1982
and © R. Piper & Co. Verlag, 1982

First published in English by Cambridge University Press 1985
as *Realism in nineteenth-century music*
English edition © Cambridge University Press 1985

Printed in Great Britain at the University Press, Cambridge

Library of Congress catalogue card number: 84–28503

British Library Cataloguing in Publication Data
Dahlhaus, Carl
Realism in nineteenth-century music.
1. Realism in music – History and criticism
– 19th century
I. Title   II. Musikalischer Realismus. *English*
780′.903′4   ML196

ISBN 0 521 26115 5 hard covers
ISBN 0 521 27841 4 paperback

Contents

Translator's note

'Geistesgeschichte' can be translated literally as 'history of spirit', 'Geist' being understood in the Hegelian sense which is similarly implied in the notion of 'Zeitgeist' or spirit of the age. As a concept adopted by cultural historians (predominantly in Germany during the period 1920–50), Geistesgeschichte thus refers to the way in which cultural phenomena became subsumed under, and thereby seen as direct manifestations of, a single, all-pervading Zeitgeist peculiar to the epoch in question.

1

Introduction

Since the downfall of the approach to cultural history known as Geistesgeschichte – a downfall all the more irreversible for having occurred without fuss or controversy, like overnight bankruptcy – wrangling over the definition of terms such as 'baroque', 'romanticism' or 'realism' has the appearance of an obsolete activity, scarcely worth the effort for a serious scholar. The lazy compromise whereby these now questionable expressions continue to be used but are kept at a safe distance by being placed between imaginary quotation marks – no need to use real ones because they are so much taken for granted – has become a firmly entrenched habit among music historians, one of those countless provisional measures which are as indispensable as they are questionable. We use a discredited nomenclature and placate our scholarly consciences with the plea that it is always subject to recall.

All the same, rather than remain in an inconclusive state where, to put it bluntly, philosophical nominalism is misused to excuse terminological slovenliness, it might be possible and by no means futile to take up a debate broken off when Geistesgeschichte was renounced, and to demonstrate in justification that it can still be conducted – with altered premises and having got rid of the awkward Zeitgeist hypothesis. 'Realism' is not a bad subject for an investigation of the advantages and disadvantages of stylistic concepts which have their foundations in the history of ideas (Ideengeschichte), precisely because it was a term which was ignored and pushed into the background by the adherents of Geistesgeschichte. They interpreted the nineteenth century *en bloc* as the age of romanticism in music, although strictly speaking the concept of a unifying Zeitgeist, permeating every level and area of a culture, positively demanded the construction of a notion of musical realism. (Among music historians of the Geistesgeschichte school, only Hans Albrecht seems to have been consistent enough to declare openly, if without further

1

comment, that 'the so-called neo-romanticism, to which Berlioz, Liszt and Wagner too were customarily assigned, was nothing other than the musical realism of the nineteenth century'.)[1]

The *modus operandi* derived from the premisses of Geistes-geschichte may be dead and buried (though it would be rash to suppose that the problems left behind by it can be solved by being forgotten or swept under the carpet); on the other hand in recent decades the counterpart of idealism, historical materialism, which claims to turn Geistesgeschichte the other way up (from its head on to its feet, as Marx put it) has been granted a monopoly in the discussion of realism in music in both the aesthetic and the historical aspects. And although, in an enquiry whose subject is realism in the music of the nineteenth century (more specifically, 1814–1914), it would be quite in order to avoid the complex and often tiresome issues associated with socialist realism altogether, it may not be entirely superfluous at least to sketch an outline of the theory, for the picture any age forms of a section of the past is never totally independent of the controversies of its own time, in which it seeks to ascertain the nature of its own historical essence. There is a danger that (since every historian is also a child of his own time) historical judgements will be based indis-criminately and uncritically on the norms we all (necessarily) use to orientate ourselves in our own time. The best way to avoid or at least reduce the danger is to recognize it and thus seek to neutralize it, instead of allowing it to seep into the investigation of a past epoch in the form of implicit assumptions.

In exploring the theory of socialist realism, as formulated in the 1930s and incessantly modified ever since, it would be easy never to get beyond abstract discussions of shadowy dictionary definitions. If we are to grasp its concrete significance, we must surely analyse it first and foremost in its function as an instrument of socio-political interests. (The fact that there is an interest behind an idea does not, in principle, either diminish or enhance the substance of fact and truth contained in the idea; the logical standing of a truth is not altered by the truth's being of more benefit to one side in an argument than another.) But if, on the other hand, our goal is to formulate a concept of realism which is valid within the context of the history of the arts and has special reference to the later nineteenth century, then we can discuss the features regarded as basic to and characteristic of socialist realism, whether in the field of aesthetics in general or of music in particular, from the point of view of what remains in the way of tangible and functioning criteria of realism after the argumentational processes of ideological criticism on the one hand and historical theory on the other have finished their mutual illumination of each other.

1. Any musical realism, whether 'socialist' or 'bourgeois', presupposes the existence of a heteronomous aesthetics; one where content takes precedence over form: this is so self-evident that it would scarcely need to be stated were it not that the fact that the doctrine of socialist realism has normative functions to fulfil has had consequences which distort the historiographical outline. Socialist realists are inclined to decry the simple description of a state of affairs as 'objectivism' (as if the addition of a pejorative suffix was an argument in itself). The polemic against an autonomous aesthetic, one where form takes precedence over content, can take one of two lines: it either denies the existence of autonomous music, in flat contradiction of self-evident facts, by exploiting the double meaning of the word to prove the 'functionalism' of the apparently autonomous, or else, while admitting the existence of autonomous music, condemns it as pernicious. And this polemic, in either form, is obviously the inescapable complement of a proclamation of musical realism, an apologia which takes an aesthetic 'order of the day' as its starting-point and scrutinizes history for good and bad tendencies. It blinds its proponent to the simple fact that in the later nineteenth century the two aesthetics, as represented by Hanslick (*Vom Musikalisch-Schönen*, 1854) and Wagner (*Oper und Drama*, 1851), existed side by side; but the historian, if he makes the honest attempt to be descriptive, is not permitted to measure the one tendency by the criteria of the other. Yet it seems that socialist realists, even when they are being historians, never relinquish their didactic habits.

2. That socialist realism proceeds from 'historicist' premises (I use the adjective in no pejorative sense) is a peculiarity which it shares with the bourgeois realism of the nineteenth century (and which is characteristic of the nineteenth century, by contrast with the 'realisms' of the art and literature of earlier epochs, whether of the late classical era or of the Renaissance). The postulate that the reality which is depicted in realist art ought to be perceived and represented as something determined by history and capable of alteration by history, dates from the Vormärz, the years preceding the outbreak of revolution in Germany in March 1848, when a socio-political commitment met

and mingled with the legacy of Hegelianism, which looked for the essence of all phenomena in their history. The historical interpretation of social and aesthetic phenomena replaced the 'natural' interpretation which had previously been dominant but now came under suspicion of being 'mythical', in other words untrue. From the late 1830s onwards it was not the 'nature of things' but their 'historical conditionality' – understood to be intrinsic substance rather than accidental circumstance – which was regarded as the decisive yardstick of a statement with aspirations to realism. And the specific essence of reality was sought in the processes whereby it alters, rather than in its circumstances, which are apparently permanent or recurrent. The realism of the nineteenth century – and in this respect the twentieth-century socialist variant or assimilated form of the phenomenon differed little if at all – was not 'naturalism' but 'historicism'.

3. Although it was Friedrich Engels (in the draft of a letter to Margaret Harkness, April 1888) who first formulated the idea that the representation of a character, whether in literature or in music, ought to centre on what is 'socially typical' about the person and the situation, the requirement is one of those awkward Marxist aesthetic maxims which are wide open to ideological misuse. The bureaucrat who has administrative responsibility for the arts without ever exposing himself to the experiences art transmits will never have any real difficulty in disposing of the representation of a piece of reality which he would like to banish from public consciousness, on the grounds that it is 'not typical'. There is no shortage of interpretations of the postulate of the 'socially typical' which have greater claims to academic respectability than that, and can be seen to take their orientation from phenomena which are patently connected with the fundamental structure of a society, rather than being apparently accidental or peripheral. At such a level, 'socially typical' indicates that reality should not simply be 'depicted' unthinkingly; its representation should be so structured that its underlying preconditions and its consequences are unmistakable and plain to see. Not infrequently, however, the possibility of different levels of interpretation provides the hackneyed use of 'socially typical' in everyday currency, where it does ideological service, with the cover of intellectual legitimacy. It would be less damaging to make a plain distinction between naive realism and considered thought-out realism than to use an equivocal vocabulary which

oscillates between the language of the academic and that of the administrator. Moreover, as I hope to demonstrate, a realism which is not exhausted in 'pictorial' reproduction but extends to the reconstruction of whole contexts of significative and functional nexuses offers the prospect of a music which aspires to perceive and to transmit the substance of a reality beyond the narrow boundaries of Tonmalerei.

4. The moral political commitment, without which Marxist aesthetics would not be what it is, was characteristic of Russian nineteenth-century realism, in which socialist realism had its roots, but it is not characteristic of realism *per se*. Realism in art implies an element of rebellion, that is, the representation of real phenomena which were previously excluded from the domain of art is felt to be particularly and emphatically realistic. From there it is only a short step to association with a moral political engagement, because the reality which has previously been banned for aesthetic reasons is simultaneously almost always a socially disturbing one. The association is not absolutely inevitable, however. The realist exploration of levels of subject matter previously regarded as unfit for art can also be motivated by purely 'aestheticist' considerations, as witness the novel *Germinie Lacerteux* by Edmond and Jules de Goncourt. The representation of repulsive, ugly and pathological features is not undertaken in order to stir the social conscience of the reading public in such a case – if morality plays a role at all it is subsidiary – but because it offers stylistic stimuli which introduce an unfamiliar colouration into art and thereby – according to the premiss that only what is novel is aesthetically authentic – justify the claim that it is in fact art. Even when the realism can be shown to be motivated by aesthetics rather than moral political reasons, there is no cause to withhold the epithet; whether an author is filled with compassion or outrage, or, like Gustave Flaubert, withdraws into 'impassibilité', has little or no relevance to the realist character of his work.

5. The dispute over 'partiality', a labyrinth of partly involuntary, partly deliberate misunderstandings, can, it would appear, be reduced to the one issue of what conclusions should be drawn from the scarcely disputable fact that historical judgements – and even historical descriptions – are never entirely independent of the categories whereby the author perceives and interprets his own time: its preconditions, its present structures and its prospects. If partiality can be justified by the argument that no one

can escape his own situation, and therefore the historian, too, should acknowledge his situation rather than seek to deny it, then partiality can in turn be repudiated with the postulate that the reflection of one's own 'innate' prejudices is a means of neutralizing them or at least of diminishing their immediate pressure. In other words, self-reflection serves either to consolidate and accentuate or to limit and qualify. It is an instrument either of affirmation or of doubt.

6. The concept of the 'socially typical' and the principle of 'partiality' are closely bound up with a third factor, the requirement that a work of art must display a 'perspective' if the representation is to count as 'realist'. (Lack of perspective, and hence a shortfall in factual substance and truth, is the most common Marxist charge brought against realism whose verisimilitude cannot be refuted by any other means.) If – according to Kant – a fact is always a fact formed categorially by a human consciousness, and if furthermore – according to Marx – the consciousness of human beings is dependent on their social existence, it follows that what is judged to be a fact is determined or coloured by the position which the person making the judgement occupies in society – a society which must be understood as a nexus of functions and a process of development. In other words: reality is always perceived in a perspective, and which of the concurrently contesting perspectives will prove in the end to be correct cannot be decided logically but only pragmatically: by the establishment in power of a form of society which will have succeeded in asserting its own particular perspective as the truth. The precept that truth is always the victors' truth is thus not repudiated by Marxism but merely projected into the future which Marxism sees as belonging to it.

7. There was always a minority among the adherents of the doctrine of socialist realism – from Lunacharsky to Brecht and Eisler – who possessed enough knowledge and understanding of art to recognize that it was not an established style and could have no kind of pretension to be a norm but, in any reasonable and liberal interpretation, must tolerate the existence under one roof of some extremely various methods of mastering reality by artistic means. It is a belief that was continually emphasized and demonstrated by example, but its degree of acceptance varied. The next step, however – given a dogma whose claims to universal validity were not to be shaken – has been the tendency to formulate and define it in terms sufficiently comprehensive and

capacious to accommodate diverging methods; but for all the merits of this as a strategy for artistic survival it has resulted in a concept of realism which is almost unusable for the purposes of art history. In the cut and thrust of aesthetic debate it was an advantage to be able to dissolve into the unspecific and the limitless, but it has been an obstacle to historiography. The conception of realism held by Brecht and Eisler was motivated first and foremost by tactical considerations, and has little or nothing to contribute to an attempt to understand the nineteenth century.

8. The Leninist principle that art should be 'a mirror', which is a central dogma weighing on the aesthetic theory of socialist realism, would be wholly unexceptionable as a doctrine if, firstly, it was not accompanied by the arrogant claim of being the only principle necessary in the interpretation of art as a whole – or 'true art' at least – and, secondly, if it had not been inextricably bound by Lenin to an obscurantist polemic against the 'irrationality' and 'obfuscation' of symbolism. The result was that Marxists who felt themselves to be Leninists but were not inimical to art have had to expend immense quantities of ingenuity in order to smuggle an atom of reason into a trivial argument they were not permitted to contradict.

Out of the fact that the concept of 'mirroring' is obviously too limiting to serve as the foundation for an aesthetics with pretensions to universality – a failing which is especially conspicuous with regard to the aesthetics of music – there has grown an interminable controversy: either art is governed entirely by the laws deriving from the obscurantist conception of its duty to 'mirror', or else a certain tolerance of the avant-garde leads to the situation where that same conception, although impossible to abandon altogether, is stretched and thinned to the point where it is no longer recognizable.[2] As a result the category is either rigidly exact and menacing or empty and harmless, according to the state of cultural policies.

While the concept of 'mirroring' was thus a function of the policies it had to serve, on the other hand the disapproval of symbolism inherited from Lenin distorted the depiction of the relationships which exist between music and reality. (The disapproval led in the end, incidentally, to the adoption of a complicated linguistic nomenclature in order to avoid speaking of symbolism in respect of simple musical facts.) Without some reference to symbolism, as understanding of it has developed in the Hegelian, neo-Kantian phenomenological and psychological

aesthetics of the nineteenth and twentieth centuries, it is
absolutely impossible to interpret the procedures and techniques
whereby (1) acoustic phenomena of the physical world, (2) pro-
gressions and developmental processes, (3) spiritual and
emotional states and processes, (4) language and its 'cadenced
interjections' (Hegel) and (5) natural or social principles of order
assume audible shape in musical structures, except at the cost of
self-imposed regression into banality. (Some Marxist aesthetic
theorists take the escape route of equipping the concept of the
'picture', which is counted as unexceptionable, with the most
essential components of the taboo theory of symbolism, in order
to avoid the consequences of Lenin's philosophical obscuran-
tism, his lack of comprehension of Helmholtz's theory of signs.)

The theory of 'abstract mirroring'[3] – that is, the idea that
music as a form or structure can be a depiction of natural or social
orders – goes back to Pythagoreanism. It undoubtedly represents
the most extreme point to which the category can be stretched,
and for Marxists who are more liable to attack than to accept
'absolute' music it is as suspect as, from another point of view, it
is apparently ill-suited to be the foundation of a concept of
realism specific enough to include historically delimited trends.

It is clear, however, that T. W. Adorno's practice of interpret-
ing music in terms of social history is based on a variant of the
theory of 'abstract mirroring' which replaces the suspect
Platonic–Pythagorean theory that musical forms 'depict' natural
or social order with the concept of 'negative dialectics'. For
example, the music of Beethoven (more precisely, that of the
'middle period') is interpreted by Adorno as an expression in
sound of fundamental categories which simultaneously sustain
the functional nexus of society.

In Beethoven's music, for all the idealism of its tone and posture, the
essence of society, for which he speaks as viceroy of the total entity,
becomes the essence of music itself. Both are comprehensible in the
interior of the works alone, not in mere depiction. The central
categories of the artistic construction can be translated into social ones.

In the analysis of details, admittedly, the threads that are sup-
posed to construct a dialectical model get crossed, for it is left
unclear whether, in order to extract a social utterance from
Beethoven's thematic-motivic working, Adorno starts from the
premiss that a perfectly functioning economic-social system will
issue out of the clash of egoisms, or from the totally opposing

idea that in a 'managed world' individuals shrink to the sum
of the functions which they have to fulfil to keep the clockwork
of society running.

What we call Beethoven's thematic working is the mutual abrasion of
antitheses, of individual interests; the totality, the whole, which governs
the chemism of his work is not an overriding concept schematically sub-
suming the various elements; it is the epitome of both that thematic
work and its outcome, the finished composition. The tendency is, as far
as possible, to dequalify the natural material with which the working
occupies itself; the motivic germs, the particular matter to which each
movement attaches itself, are themselves identical with the general:
they are formulas of tonality, reduced to nothingness on their own
account, and as much preformed by the totality as the individual is in
individualistic society.[4]

Georg Lukács, finally, attempted to bracket the Leninist
'mirror' principle with the popular and romantic aesthetic maxim
that music is the expression of emotions, by means of a philo-
logically somewhat unsound reference to Aristotle, designating
music as 'double mimesis': reality is depicted in emotions, and
emotions in turn are depicted in music. But although the simplicity of this thesis makes it highly attractive, it comes to grief on
its very universality of application: it receives far too much
heterogeneous matter in its embrace, and therefore serves to
explain virtually nothing.

Given the intention of examining, analysing and establishing
facts about the nature of musical realism as a characteristic
phenomenon of nineteenth-century art, then clearly Marxist
theory, condemning any avant-garde tendencies on the one hand
and burdening itself on the other with universal pretensions, will
hardly serve as a basis for the undertaking. Of course it will be
necessary to give as much consideration to the elementary
features which constitute music's depictive character, from the
simple imitation of acoustic events to the 'world symbolism' of
musical forms, as they have received in Marxist aesthetic theory,
although there they sometimes appear curiously distorted. But
these premises, necessary though they are, are far from being
the only terms of reference. Realism, as the representative style
of an age, possesses characteristics (the element of radicalism,
without which it is hardly conceivable; the principle of mixing
'high' and 'low' styles, in contravention of the aesthetic and social
rules requiring their separation; finally, the postulate that in the

depiction of social phenomena their historical conditioning must be apparent) which are independent in principle of the depictive features of music. Their presence is unavoidable, however, and they must clearly play a part in any definition of the concept of realism which is to be conducted according to historiographical principles and relate specifically to the nineteenth century.

2

What is musical realism?

The concept of 'musical realism' is a category which, it would seem, is as indispensable as it is questionable: we all use it from time to time, but with something of a bad conscience, because we should be in a quandary if we were challenged to say exactly what we meant. It is not that the term is an empty or meaningless one, a terminological ornament which can be added to a sentence without affecting its significance. On the other hand it is uncertain whether, or to what extent, there is any underlying coherence or agreement between the different senses in which the word is used; that is, whether 'musical realism' is an objective entity with an integrity which will stand up to examination, or merely the illusion of an object, generated by verbal usage.

Even whether it is possible to speak meaningfully of realism in respect of music, as it is in respect of literature or the visual arts, is a moot question. In the nineteenth century it was generally held that music was 'of its nature' romantic. Composers like Ferruccio Busoni, Arnold Schoenberg and Kurt Weill, none of them starry-eyed rhapsodists, all held the opinion that music is a fundamentally unrealistic art, and that therefore the concept of musical realism represents an error either in the thing so designated or in the judgement formed of it.

Busoni declared the principle of verismo 'untenable' because the only way to make the improbability of 'people performing actions while singing' aesthetically plausible was to set the action in the realm of 'the incredible, the untrue, the improbable', so that 'one impossibility props up the other'.[5] His argument was in fact little different from that of E. T. A. Hoffmann a century earlier, advocating an aesthetics of the 'marvellous', typified by the fairy-tale opera.

Schoenberg, refuting allegations that Mahler's music sometimes used 'realistic' means to achieve 'unartistic' ends, argued that music 'is always unreal' and 'tells us of the most unreal things that exist'; the means that move a listener emotionally must be 'artistic' in principle, because in music 'there is never any event which could awaken sympathy *in itself*.[6] The fact that Schoenberg proclaimed an aesthetics of the 'true' – as opposed to the traditional aesthetics of the 'beautiful', which he distrusted as being untruthful – did not therefore by any means entail his embracing the cause of musical realism, although it represented a possible but not a necessary consequence of the aesthetics of the true.

Finally, Weill's contribution to the 'Zeitoper' of the 1920s rested to some extent on conclusions he drew from Busoni's aesthetics. From the premiss that 'any possibility of a realistic effect' is barred to music he developed nothing less than the dramaturgy of *Die Dreigroschenoper*, which for him emerged from the dialectic between 'realistic action' and 'unrealistic music'.[7] In as much as the music stands 'contrapuntally' to the text, instead of 'tautologically' repeating the text in another language, it participates in the truth of the work through its very 'anti-realism': it stands for a reality which proves an illusion and the nature of whose being – or non-being – is expressed by the text.

Yet in spite of the mistrust which the concept of musical realism encounters among composers whose aesthetic ideas have been determined directly or indirectly by the idea of absolute music, the expression has gradually established itself, to the point where it is ripe for analysis. The reason why this is so may be the fact that the term is central to the discussion of a number of unsolved problems: how closely those problems are associated with each other is not yet clear, but it will be worthwhile examining them even if it emerges finally that the connection is not as close as the use of the same expression in relation to them has suggested.

The custom of classifying the music of the entire nineteenth century, from the first decades to the last, as 'romantic' is widespread and well established. Yet in the history of literature and

the visual arts the second half of the century is equally habitually
referred to as an age of realism, which gives pause for thought on
the historico-philosophical significance of the musical anomaly,
and urges the abandonment, or at least the modification, of the
principle of the inner unity of the epoch – regardless of whether
belief in that unity stems, in the last resort, from the history of
ideas or from social history. The notion of a romantic art flourish-
ing in a realist age contradicts the idea of a Zeitgeist which is of
the same nature in all the arts. (Even in Marxist aesthetics and
historiography the principle of the Zeitgeist is not denied but
merely turned 'from its head on to its feet'.) The problem represented by that contradiction will not be solved satisfactorily if
it is crudely conceived in terms simply of a confrontation between
romantic music and realist literature. For undoubtedly there was
romantic literature side by side with the dominant realist school
in the second half of the nineteenth century, and there was realist
music, even if it was overshadowed by romantic music. But the
romantic literature of the age of realism represented the tradition
of decline – examples from German literature, if required, can be
found in some of the poems which owe their survival to the fact
that Brahms set them as Lieder – and the 'dissimultaneity',
in historico-philosophical terms, of this literature is manifested in
its aesthetic inconsistency. The remarkable thing about the
romantic music of the same half-century, by contrast, is not the
fact that it existed at all but its undoubted stature: not the fact
that it was 'possible' but that it was first-rate. Indeed, it could be
argued that the unity of the epoch consisted in nothing other than
that it permitted the co-existence of antithetical tendencies –
romantic and realist – in both literature and music, while the
explanation of the aesthetic discrepancies is outside the scope of
either the history of ideas or social history, which both confine
themselves to the description of phenomena and generally shy
away from establishing norms (without being able to avoid doing
so altogether).

Realism was never more than a peripheral phenomenon in the
music of the nineteenth century: that much is indisputable and
there is no intention here of denying it; however, it does not
follow that it would be a waste of time to take those tendencies
which can be characterized as realist, relate them to each other
and seek an explanation for the curious fact that while the age of
realism found an expression in music too, that expression was so
sporadic. Of course there are considerable methodological dif-

ficulties in store for anyone who attempts to formulate a definition of realism which will meet the needs of music history. The
failure of Norman Cazden is typical: while he recognized the
need for terminological distinctions between musical realism on
the one hand and 'naturalism', 'pictorialism' and abstract forms
of musical symbolism on the other, he arrived in the end at a
definition so commodious that the term defined is rendered
superfluous: no distinction exists between Cazden's 'realism' and
what is generally meant by the 'content' of music. 'Realism in
music is the totality of concrete reference to the common experience of human beings as embodied in all the formal elements of
musical art.'[8] It may not be inappropriate, in the light of such an
example, to make a few observations about the snares a theory of
musical realism should seek to avoid.

First, it would impose an unnecessary constraint to do what
was often done around 1900, even by historians of the standing of
Hermann Kretzschmar and Hugo Riemann, and limit the concept of musical realism to Tonmalerei, or to the extreme, crass
examples of it which the adherents of a strict aesthetics of the
beautiful decried as 'inartistic'. To speak of realism or
naturalism, with that polemic intention, and to continue to dispute the aesthetic legitimacy or otherwise of programme music
under the rubric of realism would be both out of date and
unproductive.

Second, the fact that during the later nineteenth century opera
librettos shared in the realist tendencies of contemporary literature cannot simply be equated with musical realism. The
presence of realist features in the texts of *La traviata*, *Carmen* or
Cavalleria rusticana has little or no bearing on the music unless
criteria are evolved whereby an analytically watertight case can
be proved that the music contributed to the realist conception of
the drama.

Third, observation of the frequency with which realism is
mentioned in late nineteenth- and twentieth-century literature
on music is not a sufficient guarantee that the various ways in
which the word is used will allow the construction of an integrated concept, a coherent history of the term, or even, at the
very least, a meaningful configuration of interrelated categories.

Fourth, very nearly all the attempts to define realism for the
purposes of art history in general are hamstrung by epistemological scruples, but if the intention is to develop a concept of
realism to fit one particular historical period, namely the later

nineteenth century, then the larger problem of the actual nature
of reality is perhaps an unsuitable place to start. The difficulties
inherent in concepts of 'true' or 'real' reality are virtually impossible to exclude altogether from the discussion of realism (not for
nothing does the age of realism coincide with the age of epistemology, which is to say the loss of metaphysical innocence);
and concern with the general epistemological problem would be
nothing but an embarrassment putting at risk the exploration of
the historically specific aesthetic problem. (After exposure to the
dialectics of nineteenth-century epistemology, it is easy to come
to the conclusion that impressionism is the truest realism.)

Fifth, it would be inappropriate or at best shortsighted to
make the historical investigation of what Marxist aestheticians
and historians call 'bourgeois realism' dependent on the
historico-philosophical thesis that the phenomenon is a prototype of 'socialist realism': the end-goal, for Marxists, of the history of art. Every age has an indisputable right to project its own
perspective of the future, but for that reason it is not legitimate
to impose one's own contemporary Zeitgeist upon a past age as
its 'perspective of the future'. Whether one accepts the norms of
Marxist aesthetics for the practice and theory of the arts today or
not, they are at all events unusable as the premises of a historiographical attempt to do justice to the particular character of
realism in the nineteenth century. A 'dialectic' which serves to
'rescue' romantic music by means of the argument that it is 'really
realist' is a historico-philosophical abuse resulting from the situation where the postulate that art ought to be realist urges the
false conclusion that great art, because it is great, must also
be realist, so that in the end Bach and Mozart are enrolled as
realists alongside Brahms and Bruckner. False universality
causes the category to disintegrate altogether.

The difficulties standing in the way of a historiographically
useful definition of musical realism at first appear insurmount-
able. Yet, in view of the persistent recurrence of the term in
writing about music, there remains the conviction that somewhere, amid all the disparate and divergent ways in which it is
used, common issues must lie concealed which will allow associations to be made between some at least of the superficially different instances.

Admittedly some of the uses to which the term has been put,
although justifiable in their context, must be excluded from a dis-

cussion which seeks a firm historiographical footing, or at least banished to the periphery.

When Philipp Spitta wrote of 'realist' tendencies with which 'Brahms has nothing in the least in common',[9] he meant, as the context demonstrates, those elements of picturesque, historical, local colour which the literary critic Gustave Planche had called 'réalisme' as early as 1833: elements like Wagner's quotation in *Die Meistersinger* of a musical theme from Wagenseil's chronicle, which was intended to lend some degree of authenticity to the 'old German' style of his music. According to Planche, realism was the taking of pains over 'what coat-of-arms hung over the castle gate, what motto appeared on the banner and what colours were carried by the lovesick knight'.[10] By that criterion, illustrated in the novels of Sir Walter Scott, realism consists in insinuating the verisimilitude of an invented story by means of 'petits détails vrais', as had already been postulated in the eighteenth century by Denis Diderot. But while there is no denying the particular instance that Wagner's use of a 'small true detail' in his striving for stylistic verisimilitude certainly reveals an analogous tendency, it would be rash to go on from there to claim for realism, as a matter of general principle, all the historicism and archaicism of nineteenth-century music. One can admit the existence of an association without endorsing a conceptual hotchpotch.

One would be on equally unsafe ground in adopting one of the concepts of realism such as have been formulated in the nineteenth and twentieth centuries as the main props for historico-philosophical typological constructs. Defending Handel in 1887 against the charge of 'mannerism', brought by Ferdinand Hiller on the grounds of his liking for 'stereotyped vocal formulas', Friedrich Chrysander laid emphasis on Handel's 'realism'. In view of the 'fidelity of expression' always to be sensed in his every musical phrase, Chrysander maintained, notwithstanding his recourse to the commonplaces of musical rhetoric the word 'mannerism' had no place in the discussion of Handel.

Such procedures are fundamentally different from those of the mannerist, indeed a greater artistic contrast than that between Handel and a mannerist is not conceivable and does not exist in the whole realm of music. Handel is objective and realist by nature, a mannerist is formalist and thoroughly subjective.[11]

Chrysander's choice of words, bracketing 'realist' with 'objective' and recalling not only the dichotomy expounded in Schiller's seminal *Über naive und sentimentalische Dichtung* but also Goethe's distinctions between 'simple imitation, manner and style', followed the example of literary criticism of the mid-century, when Hermann Hettner could refer to Goethe's realism, and Friedrich Theodor Vischer to Shakespeare's.[12] This is the typological approach to the concept of realism, making of it a phenomenon which recurs in every epoch, but also compelling the conclusion that there must be an affinity between the antithetical concepts – mannerism, romanticism, modernism or whatever – which oppose it in each epoch in turn. The usefulness of the approach is probably hampered by an all too commodious philosophy of history, containing a greater proportion of speculation than a historian can accept.

3

'True reality' and music

The attempt to formulate a concept of realism which will serve the purposes of the history of the arts courts the alternative dangers either of falling a victim to a philosophical naivety which accepts without question an everyday conception of reality or of becoming lost in cerebrations which end by allowing the whole concept to disintegrate. In the former case realism is taken to be simple imitation of a given reality, a copy hardly worth discussing; in the latter it becomes a vainly pursued phantom, a pretension impossible to fulfil. Thus neither superficiality nor scepticism is a protection against the epistemological trap contained in the paradox that, in the attempt to place a historical study of an art on a sound philosophical basis, the premises of the whole undertaking are destroyed because one either remains oblivious to the problems involved or becomes hopelessly entangled in them. Someone who prepares to study earlier ages, armed dogmatically and unquestioningly with the sum of prejudices which make up 'reality' for the average late-twentieth-century newspaper-reader, is closing the door to a useful definition of realism in art in his own face as surely as a philosophically educated sceptic who, confronted with the striking contrasts between opinions on the nature of reality, or 'true reality', arrives at the conclusion that reality is beyond our grasp and that one therefore cannot speak meaningfully of realism in art, if one is to avoid speaking of a mere fabrication.

It seems wise, therefore, to avoid beginning with ambitious reflections on the nature of reality. The search for criteria which will neither fail to get to grips with the concept at all nor reduce it to an irrelevant and meaningless common denominator can more usefully start with a review of the reasons why, around 1850, the expression realism became a central category in the theory of art and even a rallying-cry in aesthetic campaigning. The history of the phenomenon and that of the use of the word do not altogether coincide. The fact that in aesthetic theory and art history the term is associated with the nineteenth century in particular does not by any means rule out the fact that the phenomenon to which it relates is already present in works of art dating from earlier periods: 'realist' is certainly an appropriate designation for late Roman sculpture, the *Satyricon* of Petronius, Dutch painting of the seventeenth century, and the middle-class tragic drama of the eighteenth. Yet it seems unlikely that the greater frequency with which the word can be shown to have been used from the middle of the nineteenth century onwards was a matter of chance alone, and more likely that the linguistic phenomenon was a response to a development in the history of ideas, an expression of the consciousness that a turning-point had been reached. The question then arises as to what it signifies when art theory speaks of realism instead of the imitation of nature.

'Imitatio naturae' was one of the enduring premisses of the theory of art prevalent from the sixteenth century to the eighteenth. Although interpretation might differ, this and other premisses derived from Aristotle went unquestioned, indeed they persisted with such vigour precisely because of the variety of interpretation they would stand. (The original Greek concept of 'mimesis', relating to actual representation of an original, above all through the medium of dance, had been distorted almost beyond recognition by the use of 'imitatio' in the Latin translation in which Aristotle was most widely disseminated in the early modern era.)

In music, there are at least six different things which have been interpreted, in different ways and with varying emphases, as 'imitation of nature'.

1. The simple imitation of (non-musical) sounds, sometimes, especially in its less subtle manifestations, described as 'naturalistic' or 'realistic' in the late nineteenth century, for example by Hugo Riemann and Hermann Kretzschmar. Its intrinsic significance was never very great, but it has received disproportionate attention, especially at the popular level of aesthetic discussion, partly because of its conspicuousness in any musical context, and partly because it offers a little help in easing the difficulties or embarrassments of discussing autonomous instrumental music in appropriate yet comprehensible terms. But its peripheral character renders it almost entirely irrelevant to a discussion of musical realism.

2. As well as acoustic phenomena, music is generally credited with the ability to represent spatial movement (rising and falling). This is also commonly regarded as straightforward imitation of nature, although strictly speaking it is a metaphor, for the habit of using the words 'high' and 'low' to describe musical pitches is a convention of limited historical validity: in classical antiquity 'sharp' and 'blunt' were used, and modern psychological studies of aural perception use 'light' and 'dark'. Nevertheless, over the centuries the convention has become so deeply rooted in musical receptivity that it is involuntarily accepted as a natural attribute. In other words, although the reference of the music to the reality being represented is perceived as direct and immediate, it in fact relies on a metaphor which has, however, with the usage of centuries, become the second nature of music – or has at least become the fiction of a natural language of music. Musical phenomena appear to us to express movement in space as literally as fast or slow tempos express movement in time. And to the extent that aesthetic appearances represent the 'truth' of art, it would actually be inappropriate to insist too rigidly on the difference between the elements which mingle in the concept of Tonmalerei: acoustic imitation on the one hand and the musical depiction of spatial movement on the other.

3. The musical representation of speech intonations is another thing that has been understood as imitation of nature; in this instance the 'nature' seen as providing the model for imitation

was not any actual living language so much as a hypothetical 'primal language'. Though the language itself had vanished, it had left behind remnants in music, where music is truly 'melodic', and the remnants were proved to be 'natural' by their power to move the heart, as it was said in the eighteenth century. In other words: to the perceptions of a 'feeling' ('empfindsam') listener in the eighteenth century, conventional languages, moulded and depraved by historical processes, could not wholly conceal the traces of an 'adamite' language which music was still able to make actual. That language was moulded by melody, primarily moved by emotions rather than determined by concepts, and was closer to the original, lost nature of human kind than the utilitarian linguistic forms of the present. Music came into existence as the stylization of screams, groans and shouts of jubilation, as Hegel meant by calling it 'cadenced interjection'; in formulating it thus he added nothing to what had already been thought and expressed in the eighteenth century by Rousseau and Herder.

4. The representation of speech intonations is closely and directly associated with the depiction of emotion, which since antiquity has shared with numerical theory the dignity of being regarded as the essence of music. The imitation of nature 'outside' – the representation of acoustic phenomena and the depiction of movement in space or time – can be compared with the imitation of nature 'inside', in the representation of intonations and the expression of affections or emotions. However, the adage that music is 'expression' – of affections, emotions or states of mind – is open to various and sometimes contradictory interpretations; although it is by now a wellworn commonplace of popular aesthetic theory, its terms must be defined more precisely if the historical approach is not to be undermined by the crude generalizations of an 'anthropology' which is not worthy of the name. There are at least three aspects which can be singled out for special emphasis, or designated as the essential factor: the effect on the listener, that is, the emotion released by the depiction of emotion, which interested ancient theorists in particular; the 'pictorial' representation of the outward gestures and inner stirrings connected with an affection, which stood in the forefront in the baroque age; and, since the late eighteenth century, the musical self-representation of the composer or interpreter, speaking in music of his own state of mind – whether real or fictive. It should be possible, in fact, to distinguish terminologically

between an aesthetics of effect, a theory of imitation and a principle of expression.

5. 'Etymology as a mode of thought' (in Ernst Robert Curtius's phrase) went unquestioned in the early modern period; that is to say, it was generally believed that the origin and essence of an entity were contained in its name. There was therefore an inevitable tendency to regard as simple imitation of nature a musical symbolism which, from a nominalist standpoint, seems completely abstract, representing the result of complex intervening processes. In the light of modern concepts, the fact that the word 'rule' in a motet text of the sixteenth or seventeenth century challenged the composer to write a canon is not determined by the *nature* of the musical technique, that of strict imitation, but by the historical *chance* that the term 'canon', originally merely a verbal instruction indicating that a second voice was to sing, although not separately notated, got transferred to the musical form which resulted from the process. But in the consciousness of an age which involuntarily, and disregarding the objections of a few philosophers, thought in terms of conceptual realism the name and the entity were inseparable: the musical structure was regarded as a 'natural' perceptible form of the idea expressed by the word 'rule'.

6. The contention that music was an image of nature as a whole, a mirror of the structure of the world ordered according to 'proportion, number and weight', was one of the standard arguments used in defence of the worth of the study of music since antiquity, and taken up in due course by Christian theologians who adopted and adapted many of the classical disciplines. Yet although this commonplace was handed down piously from one generation to the next, its theoretical premises were frequently enough unclear or ambivalent: it is not even unambiguously certain what the word 'music' means in the context. With a measure of oversimplification, it can be said that the definition at one extreme was represented by the Pythagorean view: the thesis that a numerical order underlies both the structure of the world and the system of musical tones, and represents an 'essential music'; this music may happen to manifest itself in acoustic phenomena, but does not need to do so in order to be what it is. What we call 'music' is therefore merely a peripheral phenomenon, a perceptible form adopted by the abstract structure which is the true object of the contemplative concept of music in the Pythagorean tradition. The opposite extreme, as

formulated in the nineteenth century by Eduard Hanslick and
Hermann Lotze (aesthetic theorists, that is, who sought to deck
what was in principle a strictly empirical outlook with a modicum
of metaphysics), consisted in the thesis that, through a structure
in which every detail, even the most insignificant, performs a
recognizable function in the whole, a piece of music transmits a
sense or a reflection of the meaningful coherence of the world as
a whole, something which evades comprehension if it is sought by
more direct means. Thus 'music' is on one side of the discussion
an abstract, ordered structure and on the other an object perceptible by the senses; and the model to which the symbolism is
attached consists of the scale of tones, indicative of an integrated
or 'perfect' system, a *systema teleion*, or alternatively of the
musical work of art, an organism, a complete and coherent nexus
of functions.

The eighteenth-century idea that the essential model for art
was, or should be, not *natura naturata* (static, fixed nature) but
natura naturans (nature in the making) means, in terms of the history of ideas, that a new principle, the aesthetics of genius, was
designated and legitimized by the old title, the concept of imitation. *Imitatio naturae*, the central category of Aristotelian
theory, was not rejected but reinterpreted so fundamentally that
it was made almost unrecognizable. Yet even in the age of the
aesthetics of genius, the expression 'imitation of nature' retained
its currency, indicative of some notion of reference between
reality and music, and this fact is by no means an insignificant
accident of phraseology. Among the alterations to which the
aesthetics of genius subjected the tradition of the theory of imitation (including the idea of music's depictive capacity), the continuity which was preserved amid the change is of hardly less
importance than the modifications which dominate the first
impression.

1. Around the mid-century the simple imitation of acoustic
phenomena of the external world (Tonmalerei) was still rather
grudgingly admitted by the French *encyclopédistes* as providing a
certain aesthetic justification for autonomous instrumental
music, which on the whole they viewed with mistrust and contempt. From around 1770 onwards, however, at any rate in
Germany, it was considered aesthetically suspect. Beethoven's
defence of programme music in the Pastoral Symphony as 'more
the expression of feeling than painting' – which was actually
interpreted as a repudiation of programme music by those who

despised it but admired Beethoven – echoed the general view of aesthetically cultivated people around 1800, to whom crude naturalistic Tonmalerei was repugnant – or at best tolerable as a medium of naive musical humour. With the aesthetics of genius in the ascendancy, a piece of representational music which sought to avoid being mere imitation and nothing else was justified aesthetically not by the appearance of objectivity and deceptive exactitude of imitation, but by its subjective 'authenticity', the 'originality' of the feelings expressed in the music. At the same time it should not be overlooked that the turn towards the subjective, as proclaimed by Beethoven, constituted a title of aesthetic legitimacy, which provided the protection under which programme music was able to flourish.

2. The musical imitation of spatial movement was condemned on the same grounds as the imitation of acoustic phenomena. Though the metaphorical representation of rising and falling motion, by virtue of the length of the tradition, had come to be regarded as a wellnigh 'natural' musical expression, it eventually became so over-used and threadbare an effect that, in the light of an aesthetics based on the postulate of originality, it could only seem a cliché. It was not that the kind of 'painting' which was identified with an outmoded baroque tradition had altogether disappeared from music in the late eighteenth century, but in the age of sensibility (Empfindsamkeit) the real purpose of music was understood as being 'to touch' or 'to charm and to touch', and if musical 'painting' was still to be tolerated, it had to justify itself by subordination to the expression of feelings.

3. Though it might seem that the imitation of speech inflexions would remain a valid principle, this was not altogether the case – in spite of the profound changes in the eighteenth century which took positive form in the emergence of aesthetics as an autonomous branch of learning. When Vincenzo Galilei, in the late sixteenth century, told composers to take the declamation of actors and rhetoricians as the model to imitate in their melodies, it was a highly stylized form of speech which he recommended; the same is true a century later of Jean-Baptiste Lully, who was guided in his operatic recitatives by the 'sublime' declamatory style of classical French tragedy. By contrast, the 'speaking principle' which was propounded in the middle of the eighteenth century by C. P. E. Bach was directed towards the achievement of a musical expressivity which appears totally individual and is able

'to touch' because it originates in emotion. The touchstone of aesthetic authenticity is no longer, as it was for Galilei and Lully, a 'style' which appears appropriate to the meaning and the social 'rank' of a text or a dramatic character, but rather the subjectivity expressed by the music; moreover, the question of whether, or to what degree, the feelings of the composer or the interpreter are real or fictive is quite secondary, because the one, all important thing is the aesthetic appearance of subjectivity. The vehicle of the expression – contrary to the misleading and trivial belief propagated in popular aesthetics – is not the private emotional life of the person speaking of himself through the music, but an intelligible, aesthetic 'I', which is as much present in music of the ages of sensibility and romanticism as the 'lyrical I' in a poem.

4. But the most obvious effect of the transformation which took place during the eighteenth century was that made on the musical representation of emotion; the age of aesthetic theory could be said to have witnessed a transition from the principle of imitation to that of expression. In the seventeenth century and the early part of the eighteenth, 'affectus exprimere' meant to depict affections or emotions from the standpoint of, to some extent, an observer, and to 'paint' them and render them perceptible through the medium of music by imitating their outward and acoustic manifestations. By contrast, the modern principle of expression which came into existence in the later eighteenth century meant that a composer 'exhaled his soul in music', as Daniel Schubart extravagantly termed it. The aesthetic subjectivity which a feeling listener sensed in the music should not, however, as already said, be interpreted purely psychologically, which would be to misunderstand it. Psychology is not – or at least not directly – a factor taken into account in artistic theory in either the baroque era or the age of sensibility. It was by no means unknown in the baroque era for an artist to draw on personal emotions in his representation of an affection, but it was irrelevant aesthetically – a private matter for the composer. Conversely, the ostentatious subjectivity of musical expression in the late eighteenth and nineteenth centuries might be purely an adopted pose, without losing any of its aesthetic authenticity. The decisive factor was not the 'genuineness' – a dubious category in aesthetics, *pace* Nietzsche – but the aesthetic appearance of it.

5. Musical symbolism was not sacrificed to the principle of expression but, under the influence of the aesthetics of genius, it

moved into the realm of personal significance: an example of this is provided by the musical ciphers Schumann used in his *Carnaval*, in some respects a private work for initiates only, full of esoteric references to the composer's half imaginary, half real 'League of David'. The motive A–E♭–C–B or, in the second part, A♭–C–B ['spelt' in German A–S–C–H and As–C–H respectively] which runs through the whole cycle, giving it the appearance of a sequence of variations on a hidden theme or motto, is an insoluble conundrum for non-initiates. And if the symbolism attaching to the word 'canon' in earlier music and relying on the presuppositions of 'conceptual realism' already needed verbal or conceptual assistance to be comprehensible, Schumann's musical code is completely 'abstract' and remote, and as hard to crack as any private cipher is bound to be by comparison with one based on a conventional system.

6. Even the abstract interpretation of music as an image or metaphor for the world order radically altered its meaning in an age which took *natura naturans* and not *natura naturata* as the model. The view of earlier times, as stated above, was that the universe was mirrored, not in the individual, unique and unrepeatable musical work, but in the system of musical tones, as the essential substance of all conceivable music (the individual work was an image of the universe only in so far as it was a manifestation of the system). It was further believed that the system of tones was not made by man but given by nature or instituted by God. From the late eighteenth century onwards, however, when a writer attributes metaphysical worth to music, it is generally the individual work which is meant (two exceptions are Albert von Thimus and Hans Kayser, who held fast to the Pythagorean tradition). The 'isolated, self-contained work', regarded by Walter Benjamin as the 'supreme reality of art', is an image or mirror of nature as a whole, according to Karl Philipp Moritz, author of the first outline of a classical aesthetic theory, because the creative artist, as Julius Caesar Scaliger had asserted back in the sixteenth century, is an 'alter Deus' – a second God, with the power to create a self-sufficient structure in the form of a complete and coherent nexus of functions. A piece of music is in some respects the equal of the world it reflects or reproduces. 'Opus perfectum et absolutum' – the expression first formulated by Nikolaus Listenius in 1537, but not part of the general vocabulary of the aesthetically cultivated until the eighteenth century – was applied

to the work created by the composer and not to the musical system of tones given by nature.

The reference of music to reality, any claim it had to possess a dimension of reality, stemmed from its depictive capacity, and this had spread into rather vague and diffuse areas with the increasing subjectivity of the eighteenth century, which underpinned both the expressive principle fostered by sensibility and the aesthetic theory which came in the wake of epistemology. Both the aesthetics of emotion, which was representative of popular ideas, and the more exclusive idea of absolute music encouraged the growth of polemical, or at best sceptical, attitudes towards any tendencies which might be described as realist. Then, when the post-romantic backlash of the mid-nineteenth century produced the realism which was the most characteristic tendency of the age, leaving its traces even in music and in musical aesthetic theory, it did not extinguish the subjective element that had grown to domination a century earlier but drew it into a complicated dialectical relationship.

There was no going back to the former certainty, destroyed by Kant along with the rest of the schoolman's metaphysics, that the evidence of the senses was enough to establish what was real, although the realist manifestos of the nineteenth century may seem at first glance to be based on some such limited epistemological dogma. Even the aesthetics of music, a discipline which might be thought too remote to be affected by the debate surrounding the 'true nature' of reality, was inevitably drawn into the conflict at the moment when music, instead of being content with the principles of aesthetics of the age of sensibility and classical theories of genre and form, began to aspire to a tangible dimension of reality and proclaim an 'aesthetics of the true'. The idea of simple imitation of nature, which in earlier centuries had sufficed to support aesthetic theories of music's depictive quality, had become too naive to sustain philosophically, because the evidence of nature – the premisses of straightforward imitation – had been swept aside in the eighteenth century by modern epistemology. And if the new watchword was 'realism' instead of 'imitation', it is no exaggeration to say that realism – far from being an unproblematical aspiration – consisted in the attempt to represent reality according to the premisses of a concept of reality which was itself open to question and undermined by epistemological doubt.

At the same time the tendency for the students of musical aesthetics to refer to dimensions of reality at all, and thus to allow themselves to become embroiled in controversies about the nature of reality, was connected with an antisubjectivism which gained a lot of ground in the mid-century. They sought 'true' reality in an objectivity which would be free of the influence of subjectivity, but under the premisses of modern epistemology their only hope of attaining it was by eliminating one subjective element after another, proceeding one step at a time along an avenue of approach to which there was no end. There being no direct access to realism, it became a Utopia, because it appeared that the only way to objectivity was by passing through a subjectivity which they sought to wear down by degrees, but were unable to bypass altogether. The antisubjective element created a negative and polemical attitude towards the traditional aesthetics of subjectivity, at the same time as its leaning towards objectivity promoted realist tendencies. And it was precisely this underlying antisubjectivism which brought nineteenth-century realism, to some extent an aesthetics of imitation which had become problematical, significantly to bear upon music.

1. In the later part of the nineteenth century, Tonmalerei was always called 'realistic' or 'naturalistic' (the two terms were interchangeable in some contexts) when it was wished to denote, or imply, that it lacked the aesthetic justification of serving an emotional or atmospheric end. Whether the speaker condoned or condemned realism, what he wanted to convey was that something more than the simple depiction of a piece of reality was involved, and that the depiction defied the aesthetic postulate which Beethoven had formulated in the words 'more the expression of feeling than painting'. Epithets such as 'crass' and 'crude' which conservative theorists felt impelled to use when they spoke of musical realism or naturalism betray beyond any shadow of doubt that they believed they observed in the trend towards Tonmalerei a polemical trait, an element of rebellion against an aesthetics which aligned itself with the idea of 'the beautiful in music' on the one hand and on the other with a concept of musical form which in its self-sufficiency and integrity was proof against the intrusion of 'fragments of reality'.

2. Using the word 'antisubjectivism' of the 'objectivity' proclaimed by the apologists of realism from the middle of the nineteenth century onwards is a way of avoiding the 'epistemological trap' and places the phenomenon historically as a

backlash against the aesthetics of genius which had dominated the age of romanticism. An epistemological survey of the countless associations of the word 'objectivity' would go beyond all bounds; it seems more appropriate to begin a process intended to lead to the formulation of a concept of realism which will serve the purposes of the history of music with an aesthetic examination of the techniques with which works of substance and quality achieved the suppression of subjectivity, the withdrawal of the artist's 'I', the 'impassibilité' postulated by Flaubert. In music, this characteristic tendency of the age is particularly evident in the representation of the intonations of speech. The speech inflexions imitated by Musorgsky, and those which Janáček heard in the street and utilized as the material of a realistic operatic *melos*, differ from the formulas of seventeenth-century declamation in their intense individualization, and from the expressive gestures of eighteenth-century music in an objectification or distancing which, while it neither is nor aspires to be 'impassibilité', clearly reflects an antisubjective tendency. To define it in negative terms: speech inflexions are not 'stylized' – not subject to an aesthetic theory of distinctions between stylistic levels – as in the seventeenth century but are allowed to retain the particularity they possess in everyday speech, in the 'prose of common life'; at the same time, unlike the 'speaking', expressive melodic style of eighteenth-century sensibility, they are not intended to be the composer's 'self-expression' but an object observed from a detached viewpoint.

3. The theory of affections, which was part of the theory of imitation in the seventeenth century and the early part of the eighteenth, was, as stated above, 'subjectified' during the age of sensibility. The denotation of 'expressivity' as 'self-expression', which is completely appropriate in the case of C. P. E. Bach or Daniel Schubart, is not however an adequate term to use of the romantic aesthetics of emotion, which is differentiated from that of sensibility by a small but crucial factor. When Wilhelm Wackenroder ascribes to music the power to gather up the 'feelings wandering around lost in life' and to 'enclose them like relics in costly monstrances', the extravagant conceit, mingling the religion of emotion with the religion of art, enfolds an idea which became one of the central aesthetic tenets of the early nineteenth century: the idea that an art which neither imitates something given, nor simply creates with complete autonomy, can be the medium whereby a reality is brought into view which would

otherwise be quite outside the range of sight or experience, and therefore needs the artistic medium in order to be perceived as what it is at all. The romantic aesthetics of emotion is distinguished as much from the baroque theory of affections as from the expressive principle of the age of sensibility by the claim that music does nothing less than comprehend feelings which are revealed to the world through music alone: it might be called the 'exploratory' trait in romantic theory. But the theory of romanticism, thanks to the arousal of interest in Schopenhauer in the second half of the nineteenth century, survived into the age of positivism, and then that trait proved to be one that realism could adopt and assimilate. Since the apologists of realism believed that 'true' reality was beyond their reach, at the end of an avenue of approach to which there was no end, they were ready for the theory that 'the movements of the soul', though they were out of immediate reach, might be detected and revealed through a medium – music – and thus be depicted as if they were elements of a given, visible nature.

4. The thesis that music is a 'realist' art was defended by Michel Butor in 1959 with a striking argument which nevertheless appears curiously vague at first acquaintance, in spite of the apodictic tone in which it is delivered: 'I declare music to be a realist art because, even in those highest forms which are apparently the most positively detached from everything, it teaches something about the world, because musical grammar is a grammar of the real, because songs change life.'[13] Perhaps when he refers to 'a grammar of the real', Butor has in mind the numerical proportions which, according to the Pythagorean tradition, form the basis both of the musical system of tones and of nature in general; but while that possibility should not be ruled out, it is not enough to explain the term 'realist' with which Butor challenges the aesthetics of 'l'art pour l'art'. Rather, the structural analogy which Butor finds between music on the one hand and 'true' reality on the other appears to consist in the idea that the concepts with which modern science tries to comprehend the natural world are not intended as depictions of things but merely as signs; the claim of these signs to represent the truth relies solely on the condition that the relationships between the signs correspond to the relationships between the things. In proportion as the depictive character of the concepts dissolves, however, leaving behind nothing but the conception of a correspondence between systems of relationships, the analogy with music,

and in particular with its 'most positively detached forms', which consist of nothing but functional nexuses of sounds, acquires a certain plausibility. Seen in this light, Butor's thesis emerges as a relic of Pythagorean thought conditioned by an epistemology which acknowledges modern science and a concept of reality which, in total contrast to the former trust in the evidence of the senses, is characterized by abstraction.

4

The 'descriptive' and the 'ugly'

The theory of realism is older than the term itself, which, although it is found occasionally by around 1800, in the writings of Schiller and Friedrich Schlegel, did not become common currency until the middle of the century, when it established itself as a key word in the vocabulary of aesthetic debate. The controversies which raged after 1850 under the heading of realism had their origin, at least in part, among the themes developed in the first half of the century in the aesthetics of the 'descriptive', a theory which, for some 'leftist Hegelians', even extended to an aesthetics of the 'ugly'. While this aesthetic theory of the descriptive and the ugly evolved somewhat on the periphery of the classicist aesthetics of the beautiful and the sublime, attracting little attention at first, its early stages form a segment of the prehistory of the theory of realism, which became the predominant doctrine of the second half of the century.

The concept of the 'descriptive' proved capable of merging into the concept of the 'realistic' almost imperceptibly. That is made clear in the judgement passed on Berlioz by Franz Brendel, Schumann's successor as editor of the *Neue Zeitschrift für Musik*.

Furthermore, Berlioz's representation is predominantly realistic, as much so as is the case with French poetry and painting. This aspect has to be taken into account, if our judgement is to be fair. The descriptive aspect in representation is the principal constituent in his work. It is only in the very greatest, most universal of artists that we encounter the con-

junction of the two chief factors of all art: the element to which I have
just referred, and that of predominantly formal, sensual beauty. In other
artists of great but one-sided gifts the two are separated. Thus it is in
Berlioz, where the incisiveness of the delineation and the realistic trappings perhaps here and there make their effect at the expense of
beauty.[14]

Brendel was contributing here to the aesthetic debate which
had been carried on since the beginning of the century, about
description in music, and the term 'realism' is only a more up-to-
date label: whether Brendel took it from Jules Champfleury's
book *Le réalisme* (1857) or from the essays Julian Schmidt published in 1856 in his periodical *Die Grenzboten* is immaterial.

Brendel could be called the ideologue of the 'progressive'
party in music which formed around Wagner and Liszt, under the
ill-chosen name of 'the New German school'. The premisses on
which his criticism of Berlioz was based, however, consisted in
the classicist maxim, formulated by Goethe, Humboldt and
Hegel, that the descriptive should not obtrude as an isolated and
autonomous phenomenon, but must be contained and subsumed
in the superior category of the beautiful. Although Brendel
thought of himself as a historian, his judgements were dogmatic:
when Friedrich Schlegel distinguished between the 'beautiful' art
of the 'classical' age and the 'descriptive' art of the 'modern' era,
he took a decisive step from normative aesthetic theory to an
aesthetics influenced by the philosophy of history, but Brendel –
at any rate in his verdict on Berlioz – did not take the same step.
Instead of recognizing the descriptive – or the realistic – as the
signature of a particular stage in history, he measured it by a
timeless norm of 'beauty in description' which took no account of
historical processes and circumstances.

Such vacillation between normative judgements and those
conditioned by the philosophy of history was, however, entirely
typical of the early nineteenth century. Schlegel, having con-
firmed the presence of a 'total preponderance of the descriptive,
the individual and the interesting' in modern art (that is, art since
antiquity), and acknowledged it as a matter of historical necessity
which no one could dismiss unless they were prepared to abandon all significance and decline into epigonalism, nevertheless
disapproved of the growing independence and prominence of the
descriptive element in music. 'Even in music, the description of
individual objects has gained the ascendancy, quite contrary to
the nature of that art.'[15] As criteria for the making of aesthetic

judgements, 'history' and 'nature' moved into polar opposition: what appeared to be dictated by history was contrary to the nature of music. And if Brendel disparaged Berlioz's 'realism' as evidence of one-sidedness because one dependent component of beauty, the descriptive element, was given autonomy and independence, Karl Köstlin, in Friedrich Theodor Vischer's *Ästhetik* (1857), on the one hand attempted to justify a certain independence of the descriptive as aesthetically necessary, but on the other hand compared the limited character of the descriptive with the universality of the beautiful:

Beauty of style does not, it is true, satisfy all demands on its own, for one wishes to discern the elevated and the ideal, the descriptive, the sensually graceful etc. not merely as components but also in their own right as independent features, but [beauty] is the summit of musical style because of its universality.[16]

Thus the 'total preponderance of the descriptive, the individual and the interesting', which Friedrich Schlegel recognized in 1797 as the hallmark of the modern era, was used in 1867 by Franz Brendel, spokesman of the New German school, which regarded itself as the vanguard of progress, as a reproach against Berlioz's *Symphonie fantastique*, a work composed in 1829. 'Determinacy' of expression – compared with the 'indeterminate intimations' which so thrilled E. T. A. Hoffmann in Beethoven's Fifth Symphony – is regarded as an aesthetic shortcoming in instrumental music, and incisive description comes under suspicion of conveying 'bald reality' instead of the 'inner life and flux of moods': realism is seen to some extent as art in a raw, unfinished state.

Where in Beethoven the poetic idea always appears, so to speak, held in bounds by the superior element of the music, in Berlioz it is too independent, too one-sided in the way it takes up position at the forefront of the work and is unmistakably intended as the element which determines and conditions the entire work. Where in Beethoven the determinate descriptiveness often dissolves again in the indeterminacy and generality of the musical expression, in Berlioz it is intensified to such a peak that we seem to have solid, tangible figures before us, but it is a bald reality, without poetic excitement, without the inner life and flux of moods.[17]

Realism is a word which serves both to justify modernity in the light of the philosophy of history and to dismiss it aesthetically.

The early nineteenth-century controversies about the descriptive were only in part a discussion of realism, and an exclusive emphasis on the particular elements which anticipate the concept of realism that formed later in the century would distort the point and the historical significance of the argument. The pre-history of the theory of realism must not be torn from its original context.

Broadly speaking, it is possible to distinguish between idealist and realist interpretations of the descriptive. In one of his *Fragmente*, originally published in *Das Athenäum* in 1798, Friedrich Schlegel contrasted 'pre-eminently spiritual description' with 'pre-eminently sensual imitation', that is, he interpreted the descriptive principle as the alternative and the antithesis to the aesthetic theory of imitation, which he dismissed with contempt.[18] Moreover, evidently influenced by Wackenroder and Tieck, he propounded an interpretation of music as 'philosophy in sounds', which he contrasted with the role of 'language of the emotions' to which it was assigned from the 'trite viewpoint of so-called naturalness':

Must not pure instrumental music create its own text? And does not the theme undergo the same processes of development, confirmation, variation and contrast in music as the object of meditation in a train of philosophical thought?[19]

For Friedrich Theodor Vischer sixty years later, on the other hand, in marked contrast to Schlegel's use of the terminology, the 'descriptive style' was the antithesis of the 'ideal style', and identical with 'drawing and painting':

Here music advances to the furthest frontiers of what is possible for it: it represents, it objectifies, it becomes epic, dramatic, orchestic, it becomes genre music and descriptive music depicting nature and personalities.[20]

If the concept of the descriptive permitted or provoked interpretations as widely differing as the idealist of Schlegel and the realist of Vischer, it would seem to be an empty, exhausted expression with little or no real meaning and serving only as a source of misunderstanding. But the very equivocation which makes the word seem ambivalent and tiresome is historically informative, in that it bears witness to the existence of an area of debate. When reference was made to the descriptive in the early nineteenth century, regardless of whether the interpretation put on it was idealist or realist, regardless of whether the intent was polemical or apologetic, it was always in explicit or implicit opposition to the beautiful, the central category of classicist aesthetics. However divergent their opinions on the subject, both sides in the debate recognized the descriptive as the aesthetic hallmark of their age: an age in which beauty, the 'sensual appearance of the ideal' (Hegel), had become problematical, either because it was growing progressively more abstract or because it had drawn closer to what Hegel called 'the prose of common life'. Interpretation of the descriptive, whether idealist or realist, rested on the consciousness that, whatever the outcome might be, the controversy as to its nature represented nothing less than a debate about the fundamentals of aesthetics in the modern era; and the modern era as a whole – while individuals might face it in a mood of conservative resignation or in a spirit of liberal enthusiasm for progress – was convinced that beauty no longer sufficed as the foundation of art, if art was to meet the demands of the day – or, more grandiloquently, fulfil the obligations which the philosophy of history had revealed as being of the first priority.

The distinction between the beautiful and the descriptive was discussed directly and indirectly, as a purely aesthetic question and in the context of reflection on the age as a whole; interpretations ranged from the idealist to the realist, and reasons were advanced for accepting or rejecting any and every point of view. In the course of controversy, every conceivable position was propounded and defended, and the shades of meaning attached to the concept of the descriptive depended on the polemical or apologetic functions which it was called upon to serve. Reconstructing the entire debate would be a pedantic waste of time, because it is the common problem at the root of the matter, rather than the divergent solutions proposed for it, which constitutes the substance of the controversy in terms of the history of ideas – what may as well be called the Zeitgeist, if that loaded term is not to be avoided altogether. That problem lies in the fact that in all the various directions in which art developed in the course of emancipating itself from the ideal of beauty – alike in the tendency towards increasing intellectualism and in the apparently opposing trend of greater closeness to everyday reality – there was a unifying common element ultimately central to the category of the descriptive; that, at least, was obvious, however great the superficial threat that the aesthetic debate would disintegrate in a flurry of contradictory definitions and interpretations.

As a matter of principle, in the interests of establishing norms and in the spirit of classicism, Hegel regarded the descriptive ('das Charakteristische') as but one part of the beautiful, which was manifested in melody of self-contained melodic design.

Truly musical beauty resides . . . in this, that a movement is indeed made, away from the merely melodious to the characterful, but within this dispersion the melodious is retained as the sustaining, unifying soul.[21]

To anyone taking that line, the assignment of an independent standing to the descriptive, even if the Zeitgeist is in its favour, will seem to introduce an unhappy exclusiveness – a separation, or an 'abstraction' in Hegel's terminology – which results in a hardening of music, an alienation from its intrinsic essence: what music is by nature and what music is under the pressure of the historical moment become separated to some extent. 'As soon as music undertakes the abstraction of descriptive determination' – that is, making the descriptive something separate from, or independent of, the superior category of beauty-in-melody – 'it is inescapably led to the very verge of straying into what is sharp, hard, thoroughly unmelodious and unmusical, even of misusing the disharmonious.'[22] In the operatic controversy of the 1820s, Hegel joined the party of Rossini against Weber; he was alienated and offended by certain features of *Der Freischütz*, referring to them as crass illustrations of the modern trend towards 'das abstrakt · Charakteristische': the descriptive separated from beauty. In fact, his polemics against Weber form part of the debate about realism: the lament over the emancipation of the descriptive from the beautiful is his verdict on realistic irruptions in the music of the post-Napoleonic era – in Weber, Berlioz and Meyerbeer. As the excerpt from Brendel's criticism of Berlioz quoted at the beginning of this chapter shows, the same view was held by Hegelians in the 1850s, although by then they used the term 'realism'.

Equal importance, furthermore, attaches to the relationship that must exist between the descriptive on the one hand, and the melodious on the other. It seems to me that the principal requirement herein is that victory must always go to the melodious, as the unifying element, and not to the principle of separation into isolated, diffuse, descriptive traits. For example, present-day dramatic music often looks for its effects to violent contrasts, forcing contradictory passions together into one and the same passage of music, there to fight it out in the medium of art . . .

Such contrasts, originating in disjointedness, have fallen upon us pell-mell without any unifying element, and the more the descriptive element is exacerbated, in which they force contradictions together, the more such contrasts prove to be contrary to the harmony of beauty: in such a case it is no longer possible to speak of enjoyment of the melody, or of the return therein of the inner self to itself.[23]

The 'principle of separation into isolated, diffuse, descriptive traits' which Hegel deplores here is the same thing as the 'disjointedness' and fragmentation of melody which Grillparzer found intolerably painful in Weber's *Euryanthe*, or the 'mosaic melody' with which Wagner, in *Oper und Drama* (1851), reproached not only Weber but also Meyerbeer and Berlioz. In other words, when compared to the 'beauty' of the classical melodic ideal of the metrically regular and harmonically closed cantilena, 'descriptive' melody – or non-melody – seemed like musical prose which, for the sake of momentary expressive effects and in the name of expressive truth, was ready to abandon the integration of closed forms which allowed listeners to take their bearings. A melodic style which attempts to be descriptive at every moment sacrifices that 'greater rhythm' without which, in Hegel's opinion, the aesthetic consciousness remains entangled in contemplation of the affection represented instead of rising above it and 'returning to itself'.

Hegel criticized the mocking chorus from the opening scene of *Der Freischütz* for the 'unrestrained burst' of laughter,[24] and in general his censure of the exclusively descriptive was directed at those features which, since the term has become part of the aesthetic vocabulary, have been called 'realistic'. Hermann von Waltershausen cited what he considered to be 'realistic' passages in *Der Freischütz* in his book about the opera (1920): Max's spoken interjections in the opening scene;[25] the 'mocking laughter of the crowd, brilliantly supported by the realistic cackle of the two oboes playing in seconds';[26] the folk-music colouring of the scoring in the waltz ('the realism of the instrumentation is another delight: the quavers of the two oboes sound here exactly like the Bohemian E flat clarinet');[27] or the raucous effects in Kaspar's drinking song ('the greatest realism is to be noted in the terrifying derisive laughter of Hell, where the two piccolos trill and squeal together').[28] The word 'realism' is used here of some thoroughly diverse compositional features: the interruption of music by speech in the opening chorus; the excessive prolongation of the dissonant seconds; the imbalance in the periodic structure (1 + 4 + 2 bars) and the cross-accented interjections ('Wird er? frag' ich') in the mocking chorus; the allusive scoring of the waltz; and finally the crossing of frontiers, the breaking of the rules governing the classical 'blended sound', in the drinking song. These would seem to be too heterogeneous to be placed together under one heading. But the element common to all of them (apart from the dramatic function of verisimilitude which they have to fulfil) is the simple fact that traditional compositional norms – melodic continuity, temperateness in harmony and rhythm (whereby two instruments playing in seconds for no less than four bars would be inconceivable), the distancing of art music from folk music, and the classical ideal of musical texture – are intentionally overturned and overruled. Musical realism manifests itself in the form of deviation and challenge: as artistic rebellion.

During the period of restoration following the fall of Napoleon, when the argumentation of both 'left' and 'right' was Hegelian, the descriptive, in its 'abstracted' independence of the beautiful, was a central concept for both parties in the discussion of Berlioz and Meyerbeer. While opponents maintained that the emancipation of the descriptive was an act of violence against beauty, as a subordinate element laid claim to superiority, apologists put forward the thesis that the progression from the beautiful to the descriptive was a trend of the time, which a work of art could ignore only at the cost of all historical and aesthetic significance. In other words, conservative critics appealed – as always – to 'the nature of things' as an unalterable authority, the progressives to the march of history. The one party upheld a normative aesthetics, with the ideal of beauty enthroned at its heart, leaving room for the descriptive only on the periphery; the other allied itself with an aesthetic theory originating in the philosophy of history, which favoured an evolutionary scheme of things wherein one paradigm gave way to the next. (There was also a body of thought which cut across the party lines, accepting that the era of art had indeed ended, as Heine proclaimed, but in a spirit of resignation rather than joy.)

If on the other hand the rebellion against the hegemony of the beautiful was an anti-classicist manifestation, every defence of the descriptive – the 'abstracted', autonomous descriptive – fired off a polemical shot at the ideal of absolute music, that is, at a principle which was romantic in origin. And in the move away from the metaphysical theories of instrumental music developed by Wackenroder, Tieck, E. T. A. Hoffmann and Schopenhauer, the aesthetics of the descriptive can be seen as a component of the anti-romanticism of realistic theory. Ludwig Tieck had represented the 'pure poetry' of absolute instrumental music as the antithesis of narrative and description:

Symphonies . . . unveil the most profound enigmas in enigmatic language, they are not dependent on any laws of probability, they have no need to adhere to a story or characters, they abide in their own purely poetic world.[29]

A return to the descriptive, on the other hand, such as took place around 1830, sprang from a rejection of the idea of absolute music, which was felt to be enthusiasm, Schwärmerei, a desire to allow the musically determinate to dissolve in a poeticizing indeterminacy. 'Such are the contradictions and nonsense in which will end all those who, forever extolling the sublime incomprehensibility and the dark, super-terrestrial yearning of music' – there is no mistaking the dig here at E. T. A. Hoffmann's writing about Beethoven – 'regard beauty in description as something more or less extraneous and inessential to the musical ideal.'[30] In spite of the idealist terminology, the advocacy of the clearly outlined and plainly expressed, as against the indefinable and the evasive, represented a tendency of that period (around 1830) which also allowed a realist interpretation. At all events, attempts to give a more precise definition of the difference between descriptive and 'purely poetic' instrumental music often had recourse to the term 'realistic', although it is by no means always obvious at first glance that the features justifying its use are different aspects of the same thing.

The simplistic equating of 'realistic' and 'programmatic' – as if music's only hope of making contact with reality lay in attaching itself to a piece of poetry or prose – is too primitive to make discussing the instances where it is propounded worthwhile. Nevertheless, up until the first decade of the twentieth century the dichotomy of beauty (a matter of form) and description in music (related to programmatic content) remained the categorial model to which the term 'realistic', adopted from literary theory, was referred to automatically. 'Here' – in the closing scene of Richard Strauss's *Salome* – ' "description" and "realism" were not enough, here "beautiful" music was called for, or rather what present-day audiences understand as such.'[31] (The inverted commas betray the incipient obsolescence of the terminology.)

Romain Rolland makes a more subtle distinction in a passage about Strauss's *Tod und Verklärung*, where he takes up the term 'realism', used with polemical intent by a hostile critic, in order to argue the diametrically opposite case, namely that the explicit programme is inessential, and that the reality and truth contained in the work are communicated by the music itself, as 'pure form', and not by a literary commentary.

The realism of the subject: the dying man's hallucinations, feverish tremors, blood pounding in his veins, desperate death throes, are transfigured in the purity of the form. It is the realism we find in the C minor Symphony and in Beethoven's dialogues with Fate. If all suggestion of a programme is suppressed, the symphony still remains intelligible.[32]

This quotation shows that Rolland's concept of realism was coloured by his intention of drawing credit from the prestige the category enjoyed in literary studies, although the Beethovenian maxim 'more the expression of feeling than painting', which Rolland also appropriated, was essentially contrary to a realist interpretation of programme music. Hermann Kretzschmar, on the other hand, acknowledging no debts to realist traditions in literature, spoke of musical realism – he actually used the word 'naturalism', but as a rule treated the two terms as interchangeable – to meet the case when composers like Berlioz and Strauss did not shrink from the use of musical raw material without stylization; and he affirmed a connection between the 'romantic' tendency to depict 'exceptional states' musically and a 'realist' practice whereby the classical rules of style or stylization were broken by recourse to basic musical elements.

The composers of programme music always display a penchant for exceptional states, for events out of the common, or for subject matter beyond the reach of human observation or experience . . . Such a penchant has become positively a trade-mark of this modern epoch of programme music: when the topic arises the first thing that comes to mind is (wrongly, but it is a matter of fact) the dreadful subjects programme music has chosen to treat. One thinks of the execution and of the witches' sabbath in Berlioz's *Symphonie fantastique*, of the bandits depicted in his *Harold*, of the Mephisto movement in Liszt's *Faust*, of the inferno in the *Dante* symphony, of *Mazeppa*, *Prometheus*, *Die Hunnenschlacht*, all by the latter composer. These are tracts where modern programme music also diverges very noticeably from the style which was customary in symphonies hitherto. In tackling the extremities of passion, states of the greatest arousal, unheard-of events, superlatives of the imagination, these composers build like Cyclopes, with unhewn blocks. They unleash the elemental strength of naked sound and naked rhythm, and give free rein to the might of the raw materials, the physical elements, of music. They support whole periods solely on the foundations of dissonant harmonies, the surge and ebb of chromatic figures, the brutish stirring of motives and themes which art music rejects as trite. The lineaments of this naturalistic style are already to be found in Beethoven; in isolated passages in his third, sixth, seventh and ninth symphonies, for example. But this style drew its chief nourishment from romantic opera.[33]

Kretzschmar, writing of a realist undercurrent in romantic music, stressed the trend towards elemental forces and unstylized basics; for his part, T. W. Adorno detected a realist factor (one which, moreover, formed a tortuous dialectical configuration when conjoined to romantic aspirations) in what he called the 'technification' of music. This process, pioneered by Berlioz and perfected by Richard Strauss, had resulted in music which was recognizably the art of an industrial age.

Music dawns as a realm of the soul, unspotted by the material world, and whenever it conforms to some extent to that ideal, it is stamped romantic. But within the general embrace of what, by that standard, passes as romantic, there is much that, if it is listened to with greater care, belongs not to romanticism but to the currents of a spirit which, itself ripening in the shelter of romanticism, is actually anti-romantic or, if you will, realist. Berlioz was a Byronian by belief, adopted for himself the style of a fantasist and a dreamer: romantic too, in a certain irrational musical gesturing. But his pursuit of the emancipation of the orchestra, the incipient trend towards technification, was anti-romantic.[34]

That the renunciation of the 'romantic' metaphysics of instrumental music, an emancipatory bid that can be called 'realist', was linked with a penchant for subject matter which, to the aesthetic consciousness of the nineteenth century, represented an epitome of romantic excess, brought confusion to the terminology (and, as already mentioned, resulted in paradoxical collocations like 'realist romanticism' or 'romantic realism'). Though their definitions and emphases varied, however, Kretzschmar and Adorno agreed on the dichotomy between 'romantic' aspirations and 'realist' musical means.

It is then somewhat vexing to find that, unlike Kretzschmar and Adorno, a historian of the eminence of Rolland, when considering the very same composers, associated 'realism' not with the musical means, but with the spirit of their art. The interpretation of 'realist style' as essence or appearance, as a spiritual principle or merely an arsenal of techniques, depended – leaving aside the question of national affinities – on the particular functions, whether polemical or apologetic, which the term was being asked to fulfil. The music of Berlioz or Strauss could be attacked for the 'crude techniques' of realism, representing a decline from classical principles of style; or again, it could be defended and justified on the grounds of the 'spiritual principle' of realism, which had been given legitimacy by the authority of Beethoven. Whether interpreters chose to place the emphasis on elemental forces or on technification, realism, the overriding aesthetic trend of the century, left its stamp on programme music from Berlioz to Liszt and Strauss; beyond the differences of interpretation, musical realism offered an alternative to the authority of the idea of absolute music.

The aesthetic of the ugly was an extension of the descriptive aesthetic, and a particularly drastic manifestation of the Zeitgeist of the Vormärz period, as it attempted to regulate a post-classical situation with the tools of Hegelian dialectic. The philosophical interpretation of the ugly was of course conducted less in the realist than in the romantic spirit: the referential model was not the 'prose of common life', as depicted by Gustave Courbet, but the Byronic attitude which ensured a permanent place for the myth of Satan as Fallen Angel in the phantasmagoria of a bourgeois age. The aesthetics of the ugly lays bare the theological structures of Hegelian thought. And in music it was the *Symphonie fantastique* of the 'Byronian' Berlioz which kindled controversy.

The January 1836 issue of the *Allgemeine Musikalische Zeitung* included an article by its editor, Gottfried Wilhelm Fink, on the 'charms of the ugly', as manifested in music (columns 3–9). At first, adopting an instructional tone, and following the pattern of the classical, Humboldtian or Hegelian, aesthetic of the descriptive, he emphasizes the relative right of the ugly to exist in music, as a contributory element, a foil or a means of transition.

What? Are there really people who take pleasure in ugliness in music? Who find ugliness beautiful and charming? Indeed, yes! And that is as natural and certain as it is natural and certain that ugliness only assists beauty to an even more supreme victory and splendour, without ever subduing it for more than a brief period of distress.

The relative right to existence, however, becomes a wrong when ugliness presumes to independent existence and significance (that is, when it is 'abstracted', in Hegel's expression). Without naming book or author, Fink quotes from Christian Hermann Weisse's *System der Ästhetik als Wissenschaft von der Idee der Schönheit* (System of aesthetics, as a science of the idea of beauty):[35] 'In the realms of music and the visual arts, too, it would be possible to find examples of how the harsh, savage struggle of the elements, and the shameless lie of horribly decayed beauty' – Weisse thought of ugliness as beauty that has declined from its former state – 'has for a substantial number of our contemporaries a more powerful enchantment than the divine harmony and truth of beauty itself.' Fink comments, with reference to Weisse:

Now some have taken this very tragically, and believed that it reveals nothing less than the fearful consciousness of damnation and the naked confession of inner depravity. You do them too much honour: that sort has no consciousness. Attention is what they want, and the sooner the better.

This suspicion that the dark side of romanticism was simple sensationalism was endemic in all conservative criticism. Art music's compulsive and unceasing quest for the new is denounced as personal ambition, and ugliness in music is represented by Fink as the attempt to mask inner emptiness by outward extravagance (anticipating Wagner's charge that Berlioz had elevated 'the most inartistic and worthless material imaginable, through the unprecedented and manifold use of purely mechanical means, to the most astonishing potency'[36]). Evidently not understanding, or not wanting to understand, the words he quotes, Fink thus blunts and reduces Weisse's dialectics to the bald assertion that the content and the form of the *Symphonie fantastique* are out of keeping with each other.

Weisse's *System der Ästhetik*, the foundation stone of the aesthetics of the ugly, investigated more thoroughly matters touched on by Friedrich Schlegel, and appeared a quarter of a century before the book *Ästhetik des Hässlichen* by Karl Rosenkranz. It was published in 1830, at the time which Heine called 'the end of the era of art' (more recently, with historical hindsight, 1830 has been called the beginning of an age of 'no-longer-fine arts'). Although it was Weisse who discovered ugliness for philosophical aesthetics, he would not, however, have granted it an independent and self-justifying existence and significance; rather he construed it, as Hermann Lotze said, as an 'indispensable point through which the essence of beauty had to pass'.[37] But the passion Weisse brought to the portrayal of the phenomenon is so forceful and impressive that ugliness – much like Satan in Milton's *Paradise Lost*, the mythical model of the philosophical concept – emerges with an almost overwhelming fascination, and seems to claim parity with beauty.

The contrast between realism and romanticism was less urgent in the Vormärz period, contrary to the picture later generations formed of that era, than their occupation of common ground in the aesthetics of the ugly, with its possibilities for dual interpretation. This may foster terminological confusion, but it has to be taken fully into account in terms of the history of ideas, because it is precisely relevant to the intermingling of elements exemplified in Berlioz. A discussion of the realist traits in Berlioz's music which detached them from their context in an aesthetics oriented towards Byron would miss or distort the significance of the phenomena with which it is intended to illuminate the subject. Only an analysis which begins with the category of the descriptive – or its extreme form, the ugly – will be armed with the terms and concepts to do interpretative justice to Berlioz's realism, without having to fall back on the elements of Tonmalerei.

The 'Scène aux champs', the slow movement of the *Symphonie fantastique,* has always been cited as an archetypal example of Berlioz's realism. The opening passage is based on the apparently unmediated contrast between a pastoral piping (bar 1), using a pentatonic scale without semitones (C–D–F–G–A), and a melancholy motive (bar 10) using the notes of a chromatic tetrachord (G–G♯–A–B♭–B–C). The antithesis is stark. But when aesthetic criteria are applied to supplement the exclusively technical data, the contrasting motives, one idyllic and the other elegiac, are seen to possess an element in common which can be described as 'sentimental' in the Schillerian sense; that is to say, the antithesis in the musical material is mediated aesthetically, through the state of mind in which the music was conceived and should be heard. The recourse to basic musical elements, as Hermann Kretzschmar would say: the use of the pentatonic and chromatic scales, though it is artless from one point of view, proves, by the premisses of the Byronic age, to be singularly calculated.

The rhythmic structure of the movement reveals analogous subtlety and artifice in the apparently primitive and amorphous. The pastoral piping in the opening bars is held at first in a curious state of suspense, as if it was a quotation of archaic music, where durations can be flexible. But this condition of independence from metrical regularity proves unexpectedly to be a case, not of 'not yet', but of 'no longer', when a view of the entire movement provides an aesthetic perspective and places the rhythms of the opening bars in relationship to the complexities of the middle section. Berlioz deploys a polymetricism which not only contrasts four groups of 3/8 with three groups of 4/8 (bars 90–1) but also makes six groups of 3/8 fit in with the four groups of 4/8 of the *idée fixe* by interpolating metrically 'dead' beats into individual bars (bars 97–9): and it is against this background of disconcerting, simultaneous rhythmic contrasts such as were unknown to music history around 1830 that the 'naivety' of the pastoral piping, when it returns at the end of the movement, is shown to be a delusion which relies on 'sentimentality' for its effect. A feature which at first creates the impression of escaping from rhythmic conventions as a 'primary sound structure' (Rudolf von Ficker) has in fact a latent element of artificiality which is revealed in retrospect: the archaicism proves its legitimacy as a contribution to the musically modern. Calculation plays an unmistakable role in the 'realism' of the *Symphonie fantastique*, which is exemplified in such ways as the stylistic allusiveness of the pastoral piping, the disruption of regular metres by musical prose, or the rudimentary 'composition with sound effects' manifested in the passage where four kettle drums impose order on the apparently diffuse. The aesthetic justification of the 'sentimentality' is that it is the condition of a successful mediation between the diverging characteristics whose submerged association is suggested by the paradoxical term 'romantic realism' or 'realist romanticism'.

5

'Bourgeois realism' and Biedermeier

[*Translator's note*: The period under discussion in this chapter,
1815–48, is defined by events in political history: the Congress of
Vienna at the start (the end of the Napoleonic era) and the outbreak of revolution at the end (and the start of a period in which
a totally different kind of political initiative was eventually to
unite the loose-knit German federation and make it one of the
great European powers, while Austria-Hungary went its own way
politically). The terms Biedermeier and Vormärz may not be as
familiar to some English readers as Professor Dahlhaus can safely
assume them to be to his original audience. They were applied to
the period retrospectively. 'Vormärz' – 'pre-March' – is self-
explanatory: the almost simultaneous presentation of demands
for constitutional reform in Vienna, Budapest and Berlin in
March 1848 was the culmination of years, recognized later as
dating from the July revolution of 1830 in France, in which the
political ideas of romanticism had become modified, liberalized,
pragmatized and widely adopted by a middle class which, reason-
ably enough, wanted a political enfranchisement appropriate to
its social and economic status. 'Gottlieb Biedermeier' was 'born'
in the 1850s in the pages of the popular humorous journal
Fliegende Blätter, where the poems attributed to him purported to
represent the views of a Swabian schoolmaster. The name became
a by-word for everything that was considered old-fashioned,
narrow-minded, politically timorous and aesthetically philistine.
In the long run the satire was blunted, and the outlook represented came to be seen to possess some virtue. When political
engagement leads to frustration (and exile and imprisonment),
many people will settle for a quiet life. In the course of the last one
hundred years 'Biedermeier' has been adopted as a useful term in
the history of all the arts, with particular reference to the German-
speaking countries, for the non-romantic art and a-political
attitudes of the period after 1815.
    The specifically German literary phenomenon to which the
term 'poetic realism' is sometimes applied, represented by
(among others) Theodor Storm, Adalbert Stifter and the Swiss
writers Gottfried Keller and C. F. Meyer, reflects the political

44

quietism of the third quarter of the nineteenth century. Professor Dahlhaus is not alone in charging it with provincialism, but this is a matter of subject and point of view rather than literary standards: it can be read with enjoyment when one is not in the mood for the Tolstoyan heights of the greatest literature of the period.]

'Bourgeois realism' is one of those concepts which are constantly spoken of without ever being defined, as if it is so obvious that the down-to-earth sense of reality ascribed to the bourgeoisie must extend to its musical culture that no comment is required; when a commonplace expresses common knowledge, it is superfluous and pedantic to ask for definitions. It is not hard to demonstrate, however, that the lack of terminological reflection has led to much historiographical distortion, analysis of which will reveal the complexity of the issues that lie beneath the deceptively innocuous expression.

When Peter Rummenhöller undertakes to map 'Haydn's path to bourgeois realism',[38] he postulates, without saying it in so many words, a connection between musical classicism and bourgeois emancipation. For unspecified reasons this connection earns the epithet 'realist', as if bourgeois symphony concerts were more real than the performance of chamber music in aristocratic salons. Yet the term is not invested with any significance, because at the only point at which it recurs,[39] in a quotation of Kretzschmar's description of Haydn's setting of the words 'Es werde Licht' as an 'act of the most audacious realism', it has nothing to do with the bourgeoisie: an outstanding example of Tonmalerei is scarcely a declaration of solidarity with the middle classes.

It might be expected that Marxist historians of music would seize on the catchphrase and define it more precisely, but for once expectation is disappointed. Georg Knepler entitles a chapter 'Romanticism and Realism in German Opera',[40] but he does not specify the realistic elements he means in the text. (As has already been discussed, Weber did not shun realistic effects in *Der Freischütz*, notably in the opening scene; but his use of them is too intermittent for it to be feasible for Knepler to label Weber a realist as such; he is thus left on the horns of a dilemma, unable to reconcile the sympathy he feels for *Der Freischütz* with the negative political-cum-aesthetic verdict he passes on romanticism in general. Too precise a definition would therefore be useless for Marxist pruposes and is avoided.) Elsewhere in the book,[41] Knepler defines realism negatively, as resistance to a romanticism which sought escape from the 'everyday bourgeois world' in 'another world'. But he offers no alternative to Tieck's romantic maxim that music is 'a world of its own' and therefore 'poetic', and leaves his readers with no guidance as to the musical premisses of a realism which would not shrink from the 'prosaic'. The opportunity to develop an aesthetics of 'the true' by a process of inference from the antithetical aesthetics of 'the marvellous' is missed.

It seems, then, that the Marxist interpretation of bourgeois realism, at all events, if not of socialist realism, is burdened with problems which arise from an ambivalent attitude towards musical romanticism as the foil to realism: romantic ideas are to be condemned, but romantic music is worth saving. Non-Marxists, for their part, under the rubric of 'bourgeois realism', concern themselves with a historiographical problem which recurs later in another guise as the Biedermeier problem. On the surface it is a purely terminological question (with which outsiders easily lose patience) as to whether specific phenomena of the period 1815–48 are better, or more usefully, described by reference to musical realism or musical Biedermeier. But behind that question there is an unexpected but undeniable difficulty that arises from a failure to disentangle descriptive statements of fact from normative propositions; the resulting confusion causes endless problems for historians, yet appears to be unavoidable.

An article by the literary historian Fritz Martini[42] was evidently the source of Ernst Bücken's suggestion, in 1937, that the term 'bourgeois realism' was applicable to composers like Louis Spohr and Carl Loewe,[43] though he did not clarify its relationship to his own use of the expression 'romantic realism'.[44] He meant that such composers kept their feet on the ground of 'bourgeois reality', that is to say that there was a correspondence between their compositional procedures and the institutions of bourgeois musical culture such as had gradually developed between the middle of the eighteenth century and the middle of the nineteenth. Bücken quotes Karl Jaspers:

Success is not irrelevant, it is crucially important. Without reality there is no worth. Experiences, thoughts, plans and hopes are nothing in themselves, realization is crucial. To the realist, it is more important to complete the smallest task, to set the smallest piece of work before a public, than to spend a lifetime in discussion, in developing principles, laying foundations, reckoning consequences.[45]

It is obvious and undeniable that if a composer writes with an eye to institutions such as choral societies, male-voice choirs, or the domestic musical circle, it will have consequences for his style which can be demonstrated analytically: it is no gross misrepresentation of Spohr, for example, if his tendency to curb an incipient romantic impulse and guide it quickly – perhaps all too quickly – on to the beaten track of regular periodic structure is designated 'Biedermeierish' or 'realist' – in the sense of showing an awareness of the reality of how his bourgeois public received music. On the other hand, it is a commonplace of the sociology of music that the public concert is an institution of the middle classes; ideally, the symphony concert is the scene of thoughtful reception, of following the musical argument; it can be seen, that is, as a fitting response to that romantic notion, the idea of absolute music, and an endorsement of the 'poetic' element of musical art – the antithesis of the 'prose of common life'.

But above all the terminological debate is only an outward aspect of a deeper debate about norms, which is ultimately a matter of allegiances in musical politics. Viewed as the antithesis of 'romanticism', the term 'realism' justifies the granting of aesthetic equality to musical phenomena which Walter Niemann, for one, classified under the heading of 'subsidiary romanticism', works, that is, of minor aesthetic importance. In other words, the concept of a 'bourgeois realism' entails nothing less than the somewhat doubtful proposition that it was perfectly legitimate, from the standpoints of both aesthetics and the philosophy of history, for composers in the first half of the nineteenth century to make concessions to institutions, and to surrender some degree of novelty and originality for the sake of immediate comprehension, and that a romantic yardstick – criteria developed in conformity with the idea of absolute music, and bound to condemn such compromise as epigonal – is the wrong instrument with which to measure something which stands on realist foundations. Thus the historiographical distinction serves to effect an aesthetic rescue operation, and simultaneously lends support to the principle held by one party in musical politics, namely that music which is acceptable to institutions can claim the same historical and aesthetic rights as music for which the yardstick of aesthetic and historico-philosophical authenticity is the degree of originality.

Another question of value judgements is pre-empted in

Wolfgang Gertler's application of the word 'realist' to Schumann's late oeuvre, in the attempt to clear it of the charge of charting a decline, the reason for which must be sought in the composer's life. Gertler chooses to interpret the individual psychological problems as if they were more general, historico-philosophical problems:

It appears that Schumann would certainly already have exhausted his capital and 'sung himself to death', to use his own expression, by the end of the 1830s, if he had not saved himself by latching on to Bach, therewith adopting realist principles, so that he was then able to continue composing in a generalized way.[46] . . . In this way Schumann's music was robbed of its most personal expression by the gradual process of realization, which turned out not to correspond to the ideal vision of the young Schumann.[47]

In other words, for Gertler the musical realism of the nineteenth century was a 'realized' romanticism – a romanticism 'made real' – which ceased to be romanticism, however, through the very fact of being realized. The historico-philosophical dialectics imposed by the Zeitgeist did harm, if anything, to an authentic romantic like Schumann, costing him some of his originality, whereas the same process was vitally necessary to a genuine realist like Wagner, if he was to find himself at all.[48]

There is a certain attraction about this construction, an example of the methods of Geistesgeschichte being put to work on the philosophy of history; but even if one is prepared to accept the methodological premisses, it has a drawback which comes to light in another passage: 'When conjoined with realism, romantic ideas necessarily acquired a pessimistic significance, for they lost thereby the possibility of pure objectification.'[49] That is indeed a convincing summary of the neo-romanticism of the later nineteenth century. But the pessimism invoked by Gertler, which can be more exactly defined in terms of the influence of Schopenhauer, is not simply a shadow dogging romanticism on its being transposed from its waking dreams into reality; rather, it is the unhappy awareness that romanticism must have in a positivist age of being an aesthetic phenomenon and nothing more. The abandonment of the idealist tradition, which is as much a characteristic of late nineteenth-century neo-romanticism as it is of realism, consisted in the surrender of the hope that there would one day dawn a 'new poetic age', such as Schumann, in the enthusiasm of earlier romanticism, had proclaimed. The historico-philosophical hallmark of the later nineteenth century was not the realization of the romantic vision but, quite the reverse, the loss of the faith that it could be realized, and the consequent retreat to the position represented by Nietzsche's maxim that art is the only reason for living an otherwise abhorrent life.

Clearly, discussion of realism is to some extent overshadowed by the question of romanticism, and cannot escape some of the difficulties and confusion attending the latter. For whenever realism is mentioned in the context of the period 1815–48, the assumption is always present, whether explicit or not, that it is something distinct from, possibly antithetical to, romanticism, and that romanticism was not the universal style of the age but one tendency among others, and already perceptibly in decline by about 1830.

The relationship between romanticism and realism in the period under discussion can be summarized as one of coexistence in the first, 'Biedermeier', part of it, 1815–30, and one of opposition in the latter part, the 'Vormärz' years 1830–48. Musical Biedermeier, characterized by the readiness (which Bücken called 'realist') to adapt compositional practice to the institutional needs of bourgeois musical culture, was to some extent complementary to romanticism and to some extent even amenable to it: composers cultivated genres which were alien to the spirit of romanticism, such as the chorus for male voices or the oratorio, but they were happy to make use of any technical elements of romantic music which offered to serve their purposes.

While the term 'Biedermeier' has found a niche in music history, 'Vormärz' creates a few problems for the music historian. (There is some difficulty in separating it from the dispute between the adherents of artistic autonomy, and the advocates of committed art; that is, between the thesis that committed art is almost always flawed aesthetically and the opposing thesis that autonomy spells ethical and political disaster for music.) After the July revolution of 1830, the mood of the age swung against romanticism, so that Heine could refer, in a rather drastic formulation, to the 'end of the era of art'; yet this change leaves almost no trace on the history of music – or more precisely, on the history of composition. It almost seems as if the sense of a decline of romanticism hardly impinged on music at all: there is no equivalent in music of the 'poetic realism' in which German literature took refuge in the middle years of the nineteenth century. If

Schumann's enthusiastic proclamation of a 'new poetic age' in 1835 is taken as a rebuttal of Heine's pronouncement – and it is hardly possible to interpret it as anything else – then at the very least, if we ignore its pretensions to speak for all art and not for music alone, it signifies that it was still believed possible to create in music romantic art of a quality which could no longer be achieved in literature, where romanticism had lost its historico-philosophical substance.

It is as if the Zeitgeist, in spite of its claims to universal influence, had somehow come to a halt before music. The view that music constituted 'a world of its own' is even shared and reinforced by those critics who made it a reason for condemning music, and whose engagement in the political excitement of the 1840s led them to regard the survival of romanticism in music not as the testimony of a 'new poetic age' but as a fatal flight from the challenges of the time. In an age in which 'all the arts are astir, straining to go forward to a great and sacred goal, to wholeness in unity', Louise Otto wrote in 1845, it inspired a 'peculiar horror' to be forced to observe

how, in the midst of all this striving and urgency, the muse of music stands still, directing her dreaming gaze backwards or inwards, indifferent to the great longing and struggle, the labour and the hope of the day.

Louise Otto pronounces her realist credo in opposition to the romantic idea of absolute music. Music

does not wish to serve a moment of time like the other [arts] – she wants a separate cult for herself, from which all profanity is banished; she does not want to know about the turbulence of life, or about her own people, or about a new age; she does not want to know about anything except her own artistic precepts, on which no one may properly hold an opinion except composers and connoisseurs.[50]

The idea of a musical realism which emerges in Louise Otto's polemic remained only a postulate for the time being, apart from isolated instances in the music of the 1840s; it did not describe the actual situation but sought to change it. And whether, as Ernst Lichtenhahn has recently suggested,[51] one considers it useful or meaningful for music historians to follow the lead of other historians, and use the expression 'Vormärz' to distinguish the 1840s from the earlier Biedermeier period, depends on whether or not one regards the theses of publicists, a few compositions of dubious aesthetic worth, and sporadic moments in works of genuine artistic quality as sufficient grounds for speaking of a musical 'realism' in the Vormärz period which bridges the dichotomy between music and literature at the time (and also on whether or not one subscribes to the theory of the history of ideas, which finds that dichotomy a tiresome anomaly).

There is a danger that the term 'realist', if it is understood to mean 'not romantic', degenerates into a ragbag of heterogeneous characteristics with nothing in common except a negative element; it becomes one of those residual concepts against which historical writers who take their terminology seriously must be on their guard. Wolfgang Gertler found 'realism' in Schumann's embracing of Bach, as mentioned above; viewed more soberly, the trait to which he referred consists primarily in Schumann's relinquishing the over-abundant intentions to be detected in works like *Carnaval*, which reach out beyond what is to be realized in the notes. It becomes obvious that 'Vormärz realism', as conceived by Gertler, the realism which could produce Ludwig Wienbarg's postulate of a 'poetry of ordinary life', was separated from the realism which Louise Otto proclaimed so stridently by a measureless chasm.

While 'Vormärz realism' is therefore represented less in aesthetic reality than in manifestos of publicists, Ernst Bücken's proposal that even musical Biedermeier – the non-romantic areas of musical culture after 1815 – can also be called 'realist' is acceptable only if one's concept of realism is coloured, as Bücken's tacitly is, by the peculiarly German phenomenon of 'poetic realism', which may well be felt to be limited by its provincialism. It was founded on a lack of commitment, which preferred to think of itself as a 'philosophy of the centre': a hankering to avoid extremes, and keep the romantic idealist tradition at arm's length, without falling into a crass naturalism or materialism – whatever that was understood to be. 'Poetic realism' hardly registers on a European scale of literature, and, on the other hand, Bücken's purpose of defending minor works of romantic art from aesthetic downgrading is satisfied by the rehabilitation of Biedermeier which has taken place during the twentieth century; in these circumstances, the most sensible thing the historian can do is not allow the category of realism to impinge on his view of musical Biedermeier. The mere fact of being different from romanticism, while existing alongside it in a complementary relationship, was not enough: realism worthy of the name had to be defined by active opposition to romanticism.

6

Realism as rebellion

The search for the recurring features which would enable a common concept to be identified in the diffuse ways in which writers on music use the term 'realism' seems at first to end only in confusion and frustration. When Hermann Abert refers to 'realistic' elements in the *opera buffa* of Mozart's time, he uses the word without conscious reflection to mean conspicuous but isolated phenomena such as the 'weaving of recitative-like or realistic passages into the melodic fabric',[52] the introduction of 'crude, realistic' themes, or 'primitive, realistic' themes, which recall street cries or street songs,[53] or the heightening of tension by 'realistic techniques such as, for example, pauses at especially critical moments'.[54] Hans Költzsch, on the other hand, claiming the discovery of 'realistic traits' in Schubert's music, uses the expression to denote an eruptive expressivity which bursts the bounds of convention, and disrupts or suspends the regularity of periods constructed in multiples of four-bar phrases with 'expressive prose'.[55]

Great as the difference between the attempt to make musical declamation resemble everyday speech and the striving for heightened emotional expressivity may appear at first sight to be, there is no mistaking one formal identifying feature common to the word as used by both Abert and Költzsch, which can be said without exaggeration to be crucial to a concept of realism founded on art-historical – not epistemological – premises. It is this: both writers refer to musical realism when, firstly, a reference to reality stands out conspicuously from its context, and, secondly, aesthetic conventions which have come to be taken for granted are broken, so that the verisimilitude is underlined by the demonstration of the invalidity of an artistic rule. It is not the recitative, the street-cry, or the tension-raising pause as such, but the recitative as an unexpected irruption in a cantabile melodic line, the street-cry articulated in the midst of the stylistic artificiality of an *opera buffa*, and the pause punching a hole in the compositional structure, that are perceived and designated as 'realistic' elements. And for analogous reasons, a melodic style which does not shrink from the undisguised expression of emotions is 'realistic' in that it oversteps the bounds laid down for lyrical expression. It is hardly possible to define realism for the purposes of art history except in the context of the tradition of a genre, and then it must be as a departure from the tradition. What is decisive for the concept of realism is not the kind of reality alone – the street-cry, the speech intonation, or the over-powering emotional expression undiluted by any stylization: it is also the form which shatters an aesthetic norm for the sake of reality.

Nevertheless, the fact that both these factors – a conspicuous element of reality in a musical context and the breaking of an aesthetic rule – are required in determining the concept of realism is obviously not enough to set historical limits on the term and specify what makes it a peculiarly nineteenth-century category, when it appears simultaneously possible to use it of detailed phenomena of almost every century. In the attempt to define the precise structure of the concept, it will be useful to make a digression into the history of the discussion of the subject.

The circumstance that an insight is sparked off by rancour does not detract from the objective truth it may contain, and so it is by no means paradoxical or surprising that a more reliable and better differentiated depiction of the nineteenth century's concept of realism is to be found in Théophile Gautier's polemic against Gustave Courbet than in the apology of Jules Champfleury, who appealed to the Zeitgeist when he might have done better to argue an aesthetic case and provide the aesthetic line of thought with a technical foundation.

Gautier's critique begins with an apparently peripheral matter, the discrepancy, according to conservative criteria, between the subject matter and the format of Courbet's paint-ings, but it leads directly to the central questions:

The notion which Courbet has pursued with such determination, of aggrandizing subjects from everyday life to the size of history paintings . . . has about it something human and touching. Indeed, why should Andromache be so privileged as to be permitted to grieve for Hector lifesize, while a widow of our own time has to confine her sorrow within a few inches? . . . We have already said that we fully grant the same dimensions to subjects from modern life as to historical scenes, but we would make the proviso that they should preserve a general significance.

A poor woman mourning for her dead child may be represented in a painting with the same gravity as Niobe, because she symbolizes a common human fate, because she is a collective representation of maternal sorrow. But if someone paints Madame Baboulard on an epic scale, weeping for little Dodolphe her last-born, he takes individualism beyond all bounds and makes it ridiculous . . . The imagination would easily adjust itself to this aggrandizement of the subject, if Courbet himself had not made it difficult by depicting the heads with such distinctive characterization and taking portraiture almost to the point of caricature.[56]

The feature to which Gautier took exception was thus not the 'distinctive characterization' as such, which he would have fully accepted in a genre painting of modest format, but the detailed and specific realism in a monumental painting which, through its format, asserted a claim to possess general human interest; this was a feature which was realistic in the positive sense, in that it violated a tradition, namely the customary assumption that a large format, general human significance and an idealized style of representation have a necessary inner connection which is founded on the 'nature of things'.

In addition to the dimension of reality which is emphasized by the 'distinctive characterization', and the element of sedition which can be sensed in the monumentalization of the genre painting, the ennobling of a 'humble' genre, there is thus a third feature in Gautier's polemical concept of realism which is crucial to the precise historical definition of the category: the claim which Courbet makes with the format of his paintings that they have a right to the position of 'great art' in the contemporary aesthetic consciousness – a position reserved until then for mythological and history paintings. Realism in nineteenth-century art is not just one characteristic among others, but a tendency which considered itself to be the dominant style of the time. And it must be proved that an analogous claim was put forward in music if there is to be any justification for applying the word 'realism' to it.

Eduard Krüger wrote, in 1866, of 'modern realist romanticism'; by this *omnium gatherum* of an expression he meant a style of musical declamation in which recitative-like passages create a 'realist' dimension which diverges conspicuously from the norm of cantabile melodic writing in regular periodic phrases; simultaneously, however, a dramatic expressivity is projected which justifies the epithet 'romantic'.

The progress of the intensification from the soberest tone of singing as speech [Rede-Sing-Ton] to the outpouring of song passes through many imperceptible stages, and the only pure distinction to be made is that between actual speech and actual song, which even modern realist romanticism has not managed to eliminate or confuse.[57]

Although he does not say so, it is obvious that Krüger is talking about Wagner. And whereas, when the word 'realism' is used of Mozart or Schubert, it is meant to single out sporadic, secondary features, in using it of Wagner the writer is attempting to encompass, and designate in a telling phrase, a stylistic tendency which is a prominent characteristic of the composer's entire oeuvre. Krüger (who does not approve of the phenomenon he identifies) is talking not of realistic 'touches' but of a dominant principle; and he invests the word 'realism' – which Abert was to use without any tendentious intent, merely as an everyday word which lay to hand – with all the emphasis of a technical term.

A melodic style which relates to reality by means of recitative-like features but simultaneously projects an expressivity which goes beyond the bounds of traditional cantabile style is not an exception in Wagner: in the mature music dramas, at any rate, to which the 'romantic operas' gave way, it is the rule. It is this factor of becoming general, normal, which distinguishes the realism of the later nineteenth century from the realistic phenomena of earlier eras. The Wagnerian principle – 'system', as his contemporaries called it – qualified as realism on three counts: by the development of 'expressive prose', it overruled or swept aside the convention of constructing regular periods in multiples of four-bar phrases; it established a reference to everyday speech or to the 'true reality' of speech which lay half buried in the accretions of history, while simultaneously it was capable of expressing emotional outpourings without stylization; thirdly, however, it advanced the claim to be the dominant, representative style of the epoch instead of merely a momentary special effect. And quite independently of whether it is useful to the historian to classify Wagner as a musical realist and therefore to declare the second half of the nineteenth century an age of realism, it is in any event sensible to reconstruct the criteria by which a style was felt to be realist in the nineteenth century. As already stated, in addition to the dimension of reality and the claim to the status of great art, one decisive factor is the element of rebellion which gives realism the irritant quality necessary to lift it above bland imitation. Just as a realistic detail, breaking an aesthetic rule, can be read as a rebellious phenomenon, so realism, as the dominant style of the nineteenth century, was still seen against the background of romanticism, and as the antithesis of romanticism. It is still negation – specific negation, in Hegel's term – which, in so far as it remains dependent on that which it negates, can be termed 'romantic realism' or 'realist romanticism'. The apparently paradoxical or even nonsensical term can be interpreted as a simple expression of the fact that, even where realism rebuts it, romanticism is the contrast-giving foil from which it cannot be separated so long as the two are understood as antitheses.

In their use of the term 'romantic realism' – or 'realist romanticism' – as a synonym for the New German school, the textbooks by Ernst Bücken,[58] Guido Adler[59] and Paul Henry Lang[60] make it appear to be an expression too well established to need definition, thereby glossing over the fact that nowhere do any of the three authors explain or comment upon it. Why Berlioz, Wagner and Liszt could be described not only as romantics – which they undoubtedly were – but also as realists (so that a grey confusion spreads in the history of music, in an area where historians of music and art are able to distinguish between an age of romanticism and a subsequent age of realism) is a question that is left open, as it can be taken for granted that readers will supply by intuition the definitions the authors deny them.

By 1930 or thereabouts, arguments centred more on principles derived from the history of ideas than on specific compositional techniques, and it is unlikely that the essential characteristic of 'realist romanticism' was felt to be the 'expressive prose' described by Eduard Krüger. In order to understand what Bücken and his confrères meant by the term, one must accept the premiss that among the factors which a historian has to take into account are those imponderables which contribute to the temper of an age.

In recent decades the principles of Geistesgeschichte have fallen into disrepute or, worse, oblivion. But although the Zeitgeist should always be regarded with caution when it is invoked for historico-philosophical ends, it serves a purpose in reminding us of the mundane fact that the modes of thought – including musical thought – which establish themselves in any particular era are governed or influenced by literary models which get in the way of the direct experience of reality, operating as a kind of selective or articulatory mechanism.

Undoubtedly the author most read in the early nineteenth century – and the author who best represents the spirit of that age – was Sir Walter Scott, who could boast of a popularity which encouraged the writing of novels on an industrial scale. It is not difficult to discover in Scott the hybrid temper encapsulated in the expression 'romantic realism'. It is true that in 1816, writing about Jane Austen, Scott made the distinction between the 'romance', in which the marvellous, the improbable and the extravagant could be indulged, and the true 'novel', which represented a segment of reality as it 'really exists in the common walks of life', but in his own practice the two modes meet and mingle. The fact that the romantic world of the Highlands and the realist world of the Lowlands are brought into contact with each other, so that the reader can witness the extraordinary without totally losing the ground of familiar reality from under his feet, must be one of the reasons for Scott's phenomenal success.

If Scott's novels thus provided an example which, to an imagination susceptible to the influence of the history of ideas, made the paradox of 'romantic realism' plausible, the earliest attempt to define the realist element in Wagner and expound its role as the essential feature of the style which stamped an entire epoch was made by Oscar Bie, who wrote in 1906 that music had become 'naturalistic under Wagner, like literature under the influence of the great analysts of Norway and France'. (It would be inappropriate to project back on to Bie the clear-cut distinction which Georg Lukács was to make between 'naturalism' and 'realism': 'naturalism' was simply the fashionable term in 1906 for what had been called 'realism' half a century earlier.) Bie supports the parallel with Ibsen and Zola by means of arguments which are by no means confined to vague, intangible assertions of affinities. Firstly, he discovers in Wagner's leitmotivic technique an 'analytical' approach in which he sees the spirit of a positivist age at work. (It cannot be ruled out that he also had Freud in mind.) Wagner's music had 'behaved logically. Its sole reason for existence was the symphonization [*sic*] of events on the stage, of which it had to paint the deeper meaning. It analysed the truth of the emotions and the characters of the dramatis personae.' Secondly, Bie finds a realist impulse, and a motive which was in accordance with the spirit of the age, in the reduction of the variety of conventional operatic forms to musico-dramatic dialogue: with Wagner, music 'shed the habit of choruses and ensembles, as literature shed the monologue; for just as literature came round to the conviction that people never talk aloud when they are alone, so music proclaimed that they never all talk at once.' Thirdly, the introduction of 'musical prose' in place of regular periodic structures in multiples of four-bar phrases was a manifestation of an aesthetic of the true which rejected the stylization required by the aesthetic of the beautiful and insisted on immediacy of expression – the unvarnished truth, whether of the tone of everyday speech or of the eruptive emotional outburst. 'It destroyed the closed form of the Lied as untrue stylization and a psychological lie.'[61]

The vague universality of the term 'romantic realism', which helped it to become a catchphrase, led eventually to political misuse as well. Reviewing a National Socialist choral work in 1934, T. W. Adorno, paradoxically enough, cited Joseph Goebbels, who had spoken of 'romantic realism', evidently in order to signify his approval of a trend which – polemically expressed – lent a gloss of tangible reality to fatal phantasmagorias.[62] But there can be no question of 'romantic realism' ever having had a terminological career in any way comparable to that of its contemporary 'socialist realism' – which originally it was even thought of calling 'socialist romanticism'.

7

Anti-romanticism

The simplest, most straightforward – and, some would say, crudest – criterion of realism in art is undoubtedly the choice of subject; even in the case of music, where realism of style and subject are interdependent, its importance should not be underestimated. It is almost impossible to discuss subject matter without falling into banality, but mere reluctance to state the obvious, or contempt for truisms, should not lead us to ignore the simple fact that there is an indissoluble connection between stylistic features of realism, including operatic realism, and subject matter. The setting up of an aesthetics of the true in opposition to the aesthetics of the marvellous was first and foremost the outcome of a distinction concerning subject matter; made in an anti-romantic spirit, that distinction gave realism a place in the development of the nineteenth century which can be precisely defined in terms of the history of ideas.

The element of rebellion, the conscious, polemical reaction against romanticism and idealism which is an omnipresent distinguishing feature of realism, is especially apparent in the subjects, or areas of subject matter, to which people were drawn. Naturally the myths and fairy tales in which the aesthetics of the marvellous, the aesthetics of Tieck and E. T. A. Hoffmann, manifested itself were condemned in the name of realism for being alien to the times; equally naturally, on the other hand, there was a demand for contemporary subjects, and an insistence that if historical subjects were to be tolerated at all then the choice must be justified by concreteness and the trappings of local colour; there must be no return to the abstractness of Metastasian librettos, where stereotype intrigues were foisted on characters with historical names but no historical substance.

During the 1850s Adolf Bernhard Marx, a spokesman for the liberal Zeitgeist, raised objections to Wagner's choice of subjects in *Tannhäuser* and *Lohengrin*, in the unshaken conviction that the future belonged to a musical drama which would take its subjects from historically and socially determined, concrete reality. In a chapter entitled 'The Future', he wrote:

But is this drama to be the drama of the future? The Middle Ages a picture of our future? Is what is past and done with to be the issue of our hopes? Impossible! . . . No. That is not the opera of the future. That is flight from the present, which has had little of general interest to offer the spirit of the German artist, into a past in which, once upon a time, when we were hopeful young sparks, weary of the everlasting doings of the Romans and the Greeks, we could at least weave fantasies of German glories and were proud to feel the soil of the fatherland beneath our feet.

The flight had led Wagner, 'who fought for quite another cause in Dresden, to a repository of bizarre social traditions governing those peculiar rights, professions, honours and apprehensions, which had their roots somewhere quite other than in the people, or in Christianity, or in the general human element.'[63] If Wagner was looking for the 'general human element' in the fundamental structures of myths, and expected to penetrate them by pushing his way through historical conventions, whether of the past or of the present, Marx held the diametrically opposite belief that it was to be reached only through the kind of concrete realism which was historically and socially valid and could be achieved most effectively with present-day subject matter.

A definition of realism can be outlined which owes something, though not everything, to French literary and artistic theory of the 1850s, the most influential spokesman and publicist of which, for all his limitations, was Jules Champfleury, who published *Le réalisme* in 1857. In outline, then, realism is (1) an – as far as possible – objective representation of (2) social reality, set in either (3) the present time or (4) a concrete past, a reality which (5) also extends to areas which were previously excluded from art as 'unsuitable', and the depiction of which (6) frequently breaks the traditional rules of stylization. Though this loose collection of criteria is not offered as anything more than an entirely provisional definition, at any event it makes plain the fundamental anti-romanticism of the concept or theory behind it and it satisfies the condition stated at the outset, that it must be possible to identify a precise historical location, if the definition of realism is to be of any practical use for the purposes of art history.

The striving for objectivity is undoubtedly an indispensable criterion of realism in art, but even when objectivity was understood first and foremost in a purely positivist spirit as entailing nothing more than what was publicly observable (intersubjectivity), it was a perilous undertaking. In the nineteenth century, an age not only of scientifically based positivism but also of epistemology, concepts of objectivity or reality were comprehended within a dialectics which left unmistakable traces on realism in art – even operatic realism, as a later chapter will show.

At the same time, the effort to appear objective – the 'impassibilité' advocated by Gustave Flaubert, who claimed to put it to use in his own novels – almost gives off a whiff of romanticism suppressed: the proof of objectivity is its antisubjectivity. It remains to be shown, however, that 'impassibilité' is not merely a psychological category; if it is also an aesthetic category – and in opera that means a dramaturgical one – the proper place to consider it is not so much in speculation about creative artistic processes as rather in the analysis of the functions of music in the representation or realization of dramatic fables.

In a later chapter, a comparison between Meyerbeer's *Le prophète* and Musorgsky's *Boris Godunov* will demonstrate, among other things, that when theorizing opera composers take up the pursuit of realism it will be social rather than private reality which determines and directs the choice of subject and the interpretation of the fable; there will be a reciprocal relationship, too, between the choice of subject and the principles of the musical structures. It is not enough to call attention to the degree of historical authenticity which distinguishes the Russian libretto from the French, let alone to make it the sole criterion. What is far more conclusive is the perceptible relationship between the musical dramaturgy – the function of the music in the realization of the action – and the different emphasis given to the private or social aspects of the plot. In other words, the aesthetic categories, the assumptions which, in Musorgsky's case, spring from his aesthetics of the true – are linked with, or transmitted by means of, categories of dramaturgy and compositional technique in a way which can be proved analytically.

An analogous attempt to show the dramaturgical consequences of accentuating social rather than merely private elements should also be made with operas like *La traviata* or Moniuszko's *Halka*, which were set in the present or the immediate past; this would help to define the concept of realism which such works represent with sufficient precision to show that it was an important category even in terms of music history, and not merely in the history of operatic subject matter.

But although the striving for objectivity and the representation of social rather than purely personal reality are essential, they are still not enough to furnish realism with a full definition and a precise historical location. An interpretation of later nineteenth-century opera undertaken with the purpose of defining realism within the limits of music history – that is, procuring a definition which will be comprehensible and useful because it relates to the concrete traditions of specific musical genres rather than occupying a vacuum – can well make use of the criterion employed by Erich Auerbach in his book *Mimesis* (1946): this is the criterion of stylistic mixture, involving the cancellation or suspension of an aesthetic norm whereby tragedy and comedy were distinguished not only dramaturgically but also socially. The rule governing different stylistic levels went back to the Greeks and meant, in effect, that tragic fates were the preserve of royalty and other great ones, whereas comedy, casting an amused but distanced look *de haut en bas*, was considered the only suitable medium for the representation of ordinary folk.

The rule entails an unmistakable assumption – or presumption – about society, and breaking it therefore implies social criticism. Broken it was, and proved invalid, in the middle-class tragedy of the eighteenth century and the rustic tragedy of the nineteenth. The rebellion against the tradition of aesthetic-cum-social stylization was realist in spirit in so far as an area of subject matter previously considered closed to art – the representation of tragic fates in a 'low' milieu – was opened up in the conscious conviction that thereby 'true' reality – not a reality distorted by prejudices, and not a reality intentionally stylized – at last found its place in drama. Through this belief, middle-class tragedy, and rustic tragedy in due course, contributed to a new prejudice, namely that the middle class, or village society, was the manifestation of the 'general human element'; initially inspiring, this dogma eventually imposed its own limitations. The epithet 'realist' was given to any drama, including musical drama, in which the lower social strata suffered fates which revealed the underlying scheme of tragedy – or of tragic drama – even when the traditional principle of stylization had merely been transferred wholesale to the new milieu, without becoming any the less stylized, or any the more direct in the depiction of 'naked' reality.

There is, finally, a criterion which has remained peripheral to the development of opera but constitutes the covert motive power which activates realism in the literature of the twentieth century as it did that of the nineteenth. This is the requirement that a realism worthy of the name depicts not just any random segment of reality but specifically an era which has previously been excluded as unfit for artistic representation. When Oscar Bie speaks of operas (by Puccini and Giordano) which 'coax new secrets from music [by means of] reckless reporting of realistic happenings',[64] the word 'reckless' (rücksichtslos) refers to the overthrow of stylistic principles which had previously kept certain areas of subject matter out of operatic librettos and denied them an appropriate musical realization. What other areas and aspects of reality, however open-minded and free from prejudice an age professes to be, still remain excluded from art by an interior censorship which is all the more effective for being unconscious? That is the constantly nagging question which will not be silenced, the thorn that no aesthetic theory of realism ever draws from its flesh except at the price of ideological dogmatization. The historico-philosophical importance of realism consists in the unease with which the question is confronted as to whether or not a realist work of art has achieved its prime objective, the representation of 'true' reality.

8

Realism in Italian opera

In any case, I don't have such a horror of cabalettas, and if a young composer were to appear tomorrow who could write any as worthwhile as, for example, 'Meco tu vieni o misera' or 'Perchè non posso odiarti', I would listen to them with all my heart and renounce all the harmonic sophistries, all the affectations of our learned orchestrators. Ah, progress, science, realism! Alas, alas! Be as real as you like, but . . . Shakespeare was a realist, though he did not know it. He was an inspired realist; we are planning and calculating realists. So taken all in all, system for system, cabalettas are still better.[65]

The irritation with which Verdi – in the midst of his revision of *Simon Boccanegra* – expresses himself on the subject of realism, among other catchwords of the time, should not be taken at its face value. Verdi was fond of presenting himself as a traditionalist and an ignorant peasant who trusted to inspiration alone, but he paid closer attention to what was happening in the musical environment in which he lived than he liked to admit.

He may have cursed the journalistic cliché that realism had become by 1880, but nevertheless he adapted to his own uses the realist tendencies with which he must have been acquainted since his visits to Paris around 1850. It may have been done inconspicuously but it was done with conscious artistic intent.

Dieter Schnebel has proposed a definition of Verdian realism which combines features originating in literary theory with specifically musical elements:

Verdi's gestural style of musical drama makes possible a musical realism which shows the real person in his real, i.e. social, situation, but also directs a light on to the inner reality of the person, his false and his true

feelings – even when they are purely instinctive or otherwise unconscious – which simultaneously X-rays and sympathetically illuminates
them: the radiance, of course, comes from the music.[66]

Schnebel mentions the concrete historical settings whereby
Verdi's librettos are distinguished from the mythological settings
of Wagner's music dramas, but he does not labour the demand,
found in so many definitions of realism, for contemporary subject matter – a condition Verdi met only once, in *La traviata*. (To
insist on the exclusion of historical subjects would produce the
extraordinary outcome of an interpretation of musical realism
which excluded *Boris Godunov*.)

The stress on the social factor, contrary to appearances, is not
an entirely modern obsession; it is a standard ingredient in literary theories of realism in the nineteenth century. And Schnebel's
description of the ambivalence of the merciless yet kindly light
which Verdi sheds on the emotions recalls Flaubert, who spoke
of the 'impassibilité' the novelist should preserve but could also
say that Emma Bovary was himself.

But the fourth factor Schnebel mentions is the crucial one: the
emphatically gestural nature of the musical expression. The fact
that the affections which move the characters in a Verdi opera
are such as demand expression in gesture – and that phrases of
the text which are vital to understanding should stand out as
'parola scenica' – is the dramaturgical aspect of a situation which
rests on the compositional fact that Verdi was before all else a
genius of musical rhythm. (What laymen call melody is often
primarily a matter of rhythm.)

Schnebel's definition of realism is broad enough to embrace
more or less the whole of Verdi's oeuvre, apart from a few of the
early works. If we wish to concentrate on a theory of realism as
it was understood in the mid-century, the obvious thing to do is
look for, or reconstruct, a connection between French realism in
the 1850s and the dramaturgical premisses of *La traviata*.[67] Seen
in that light, the opera emerges as, so to speak, a realist enclave
in an oeuvre which, as a whole, is representative of Italian
romanticism.[68] With a setting in the immediate present – a revol-
utionary innovation in the history of *opera seria* librettos – and
with the individual fates of the principal characters influenced by
a social mechanism which is not merely an implicit background
but is actually depicted in action on the stage, *La traviata*

undoubtedly draws very close to a realism which was being propagated and theorized about in Paris at a time when Verdi must have encountered it there. Moreover, the choice of a subject which made a *demi-mondaine*, a *femme entretenue*, the protagonist of a tragedy was an act of provocation in the 1850s, a flagrant offence against the classicist rule of stylistic class distinctions, and as such it represented realism in its seditious aspect.

Although the same epithet, realist, can be applied both to the choice of subject, taken from *La dame aux camélias* by Alexandre Dumas *fils*, and to the gestural representation of the affections which brings interior motions and motives to the surface, it does not mean that the two concepts of realism which have been aired in the Verdi literature – one primarily literary in orientation and the other looking to musical dramaturgy – can be said to be complementary or represent two aspects of the same thing. The alternative thesis, namely that the realist milieu meant nothing more to Verdi than a fresh opportunity to deploy the archetypal *opera seria* configuration of soprano, tenor and baritone which *La traviata* shares with *Ernani*, *Rigoletto* and *Il trovatore*, cannot be waved away as irrelevant.

The essential thing is that the social structure depicted in *La traviata* is not merely a background for arias and duets in which the foreground action, the conflict between individuals, is conducted. That the influence of society operates at every level in the tragic dialectics of the situation in which Violetta and Alfredo become ensnared is made abundantly and explicitly clear to an audience able to interpret the clues provided by the musico-scenic text, both in Act 1 and in the finale of Act 2. The Drinking Song, No. 3, has to some extent both an exterior, social facet and an interior, personal one. Then in No. 4, Waltz and Duet, it is precisely the mingling of the waltz, heard from the neighbouring room, and the duet, which fills the musical foreground, which signifies and expresses the ambivalence already weighing on the love of Violetta and Alfredo: a liaison begun in accordance with the accustomed rites of the *demi-monde* has given rise to an emotion which runs very deep and yet is uncertain of itself, and the situation induces all the more passion in the threatened love and poses all the greater threat to the passion. As later with the cantabile and the cabaletta in Violetta's aria, No. 6, the listener to some extent needs to imagine the Andantino and the waltz as simultaneous rather than consecutive, in order to grasp the dramatic truth which Verdi intends to express: beneath the surface, the eruptive emotion is as potently present in the waltz as the lilt of the waltz is present in the Appassionato.

To ask whether the contemporary subject matter has left distinguishing marks on the music and the musical dramaturgy of *La traviata* which differentiate it stylistically from *Ernani* or *Rigoletto* is to bark up the wrong tree altogether. Verdi's music is unaffected by the century in which his action takes place, and its modernity is a matter of course. Rather, it is the historicity suggested by some of the librettos, while the music makes no attempt to adopt historical colouring, which posed a small, but not crippling problem in the nineteenth century, when historical consciousness extended even to theatrical style.

It can never have been thought that *La traviata* was formally anything other than an *opera seria* of traditional cut, but that is not to say that it is of no interest or value to examine individual departures from tradition in the musical procedures in the light of realist tendencies in the libretto. Among the signs which could be read in the nineteenth century as indications of an opera's modernity – understood as its position on the road towards music drama – was the extent to which dialogue – 'dialogisierte Melodie' ('melody adapted to dialogue') in Wagner's term – came to occupy the foreground as a medium of dramatic confrontation. Accordingly, the duet is the form in which realist tendencies, if any, will be found.

The great duet between Violetta and Germont *père* in Act 2, the turning point of the drama and thus one of the opera's central numbers, moves beyond the simple formal schemata traditional in the genre to a structure built up, for good dramaturgical reasons, from numerous small sections. If the basic framework of cantabile and cabaletta is still discernible at every point, however great the reduplication and variation, that is not surprising in a composer who needed to keep a particularly firm hold on tradition when he was feeling his way forward into the unknown and untried.

In the second part of the duet, the familiar schema, consisting of an Andantino cantabile ('Dite alle giovine') and an Allegro ('Morro!'), is unmistakable, although the intervening passage, providing the dramaturgical motive for the change in tempo, is given a relatively independent existence and significance. In the first part, however, Verdi's procedure is to group the individual members of his structure in an order to some extent different from the usual one: a procedure which, if the difference was to be recognized, relied on the audience possessing a deep, long-standing familiarity with the stereotype. It starts with an Allegro moderato, expressly marked 'cantabile' ('Pura siccome un angelo'); the sequel is an Andante piuttosto mosso, whose insistent, rhythmically pointed melody ('Un dì, quando le veneri') creates the effect of a cabaletta in a slow tempo. In other words, in spite of the inversion of the normal tempo scheme – allegro–andante instead of andante–allegro – characteristics which are recognizable individually as 'belonging' to cantabile and cabaletta still appear in the familiar order hallowed by convention.

The decisive factor, however, is that within the sections defined overall by one tempo, Verdi juxtaposes passages which are extremely strongly contrasted in their musical character. Sometimes, but not always, this entails some modification of tempo, but it is clear that the essential unit of the musical form is not the larger section designated by tempo but the melodic unit in which one emotion at a time is expressed (Allegro moderato: 'Pura siccome un angelo'; Animando a poco a poco: 'Ah! comprendo'; Vivacissimo: 'Non sapete quale affetto'; Ancor più vivo: 'Ah il supplizio è sì spietato'). Certainly Verdi was not following the path Wagner took, in the 1850s, in the direction of 'musical prose': now, as ever, the syntactical framework for this series of passages expressing contrasting emotions was formed from the period, founded on the twin bases of harmony and rhythm, and relying on standard tonal cadence and the principle of metrical correspondence. (The period plays a far more essential role in creating the impression of formal solidity and integrity than the schemata of repetition which are usually named in music theory as the foremost characteristic of 'rounded' forms.)

One element that can be seen as realist is that the musical periods are also periods of dialogue. But however violent the contrasts may appear to be, the impression never arises of a mere string of emotions, paraded one after another, or of the composer following the text one step at a time; the contrasting periods always relate to each other like dialectical, mutually complementary antitheses, and their effect is therefore to some extent form-building. It is an effect which is well-founded, both dramaturgically – in the confrontation between the characters, whose speech at this point constitutes the action – and also in terms of the musical form – in the structural function of the cantabile–cabaletta schema which is still detectable, though half-hidden among the departures from the norm. The mere evocation of the stereotype, weak though it is, is enough to give the musical dialogue the support it needs, if it is not to disintegrate and be held together merely by the 'exterior' forces of the text and its dramatic structure. (The problem of 'dialogisierte Melodie' remained a crux in Verdi's later operas, as in Wagner's music dramas. In Wagner, leitmotivic technique provides the structural counterweight to the 'musical prose' which was, for him, the necessary consequence of the dialogue principle; in opera orientated towards drama, the dialogue principle was supreme.)

The duet ends with a coda in which the cabaletta melody, instead of surging towards a stretta, dissolves in a sobbing Adagio which it is not overstatement to call realistic: formal tradition is jettisoned for the sake of dramatic truth. Taken in its entirety, however, the duet exists to solve a compositional problem: how is melody to be adapted to dialogue, and how are emotional antitheses to be allowed to clash in as small a space as possible, without the basic structural unit of the period and the broader cantabile–cabaletta framework being abandoned altogether? That problem is not specifically one of realism, or directly posed by the realism of the subject matter of *La traviata*. True, the intensity of the musical representation of the emotions, like the adaptation of the melody to dramatic dialogue and the clash of words, is a thoroughly realist trait in line with the realism of the libretto. But with the instinct of a composer who was on the same wavelength as his audience, Verdi kept well away from musical prose and structures which would enhance continuity only at the expense of weakening or even abandoning formal integration. Indeed, it is fair to say that the formal problem he tried to solve in scenes like the duet between Violetta and Georges Germont only existed because he adopted some of the features of musical realism – above all the adaptation of melody to dialogue – but turned his face against others – musical prose and its consequences – because they were alien to opera. So Verdi was a musical realist who felt no obligation to accept everything he found in the aesthetic doctrine of realism. Like almost every musical dramatist of any standing who is aware of the inherent contradictions of opera – the 'impossible art form', as Oscar Bie called it – he was not consistent.

The affinity between *La traviata* and French realism of the

1850s has not deterred musical criticism, at least outside Italy, from finding the lyrical element in Verdi's operas better developed and more effective than the realist. Equally the verismo of Pietro Mascagni, the Italian variant of French naturalism, has been regarded not as a new departure within the operatic tradition but as 'brutalization', an excess driving both lyricism and realism to extremes. Walter Niemann wrote of 'musical verismo's emotionally white-hot, brutal depiction of reality':

The brutal and cheapjack musical imposture of most of these verismo operas did not prevent their being overrated to a degree which today seems scarcely comprehensible. For all musical reservations and objections were simply beaten to the ground by the brutal impact of a highly dramatic action whittled down to the briefest of formulas and the music to match it.[69]

The idea that the forcing of emotional expression is a characteristic of the musical depiction of reality – in other words, that verismo and the conventions of the lyric theatre converge instead of being fundamentally opposed – obviously depends for its plausibility on the prior belief that 'true reality' must be sought somewhere other than where we – the opera audience – actually are: somewhere, that is, where things still proceed in a savage, elemental fashion. Realism unexpectedly turns out to be exoticism. Mascagni's Sicily, like Japan or California for Puccini, is a fantasy landscape in the imagination of the opera audience, peopled with noble savages, the Utopian figures who had haunted the European imagination since Rousseau.

Thus if a term from aesthetic history, normally used as a convenient label of little real substance, is taken literally as an object for study in terms of the history of ideas, it is easy to arrive at the conclusion that there is hardly anything in opera which ever deserved the name of verismo.[70] Although the archetype of veristic opera, *Cavalleria rusticana*, uses a libretto based on an incontestably veristic play by Giovanni Verga – itself adapted from a story – the number of criteria of naturalistic style which the opera still observes is remarkably small. (The one realist feature which is undiminished in verismo opera is the rebellion implied by the 'shocking' choice of 'low-class', previously neglected areas of subject matter.)

Firstly, at each step in the process of transformation from story to play and from play to libretto, the subject moved steadily further away from the 'fatto nudo e schietto' which Verga claimed to depict. Secondly, the prose of Verga's play was replaced by verse in the libretto because, in spite of Wagner and Musorgsky, Italian composers did not recognize that musical prose offered an appropriate stylistic means to express the realist aspirations manifested in the choice of subject – or if they did, then they did not know how to make use of it. Thirdly, the action in Verga's versions is motivated by social factors and reflects a critical attitude to society: Lola marries Alfio because he is rich and Turiddu is poor, and Santuzza's betrayal is not a spontaneous reaction but the carefully calculated revenge of a woman who feels abused by having been made the object of the pretence of love whereby Turiddu only wanted to make Lola jealous. In the opera this solid motivation is replaced by a dramaturgical mechanism set in motion by abstract, 'general human' emotions, on which the social setting is in no way contingent. Fourthly, the claim that traditional bel canto is largely replaced in veristic opera by an 'aria d'urlo' ('howling') proves on closer inspection to be a gross exaggeration: although singing not infrequently crosses the dividing lines into speech or screaming at moments of tragic catastrophe, veristic opera, which is opera first and veristic only second, preserves overall, or for long stretches at a time, an indisputably lyrical tone. Fifthly, quite a substantial proportion of the musical numbers in *Cavalleria rusticana* are actually 'on-stage music': real performances of music as part of the story; but this fact is put to conventional rather than realist use. Instead of introducing 'musical reality' into his score in the shape of quotations (or simulations) of Sicilian folk music, Mascagni uses the on-stage music to provide a counterweight of numbers written in closed forms to balance the 'arie d'urlo' – the naturalistic outbursts at the moments of catastrophe. And without that counterweight it is unlikely that the opera would have achieved the popularity which it still enjoys, virtually unchallenged, after nearly a century.

But although the argument that the word verismo has no real meaning where opera is concerned seems conclusive at first glance, it does not stand up so well if allowances are made for the limitations inherent in the specific nature of opera as a theatrical genre.

Firstly, the basis for the discussion of realism as an aesthetic phenomenon with its place in art history should not be some general, everyday notion of 'immediate reality', but consideration of the degree of reality characteristic of a particular genre: the fact that an opera is axiomatically further removed from what is generally called reality than a prose narrative relating the same subject is obvious enough, but it says little or nothing about what may be classed as realism in opera. Secondly, naturalism had it in itself to turn at any moment into aestheticism, and to depict a segment of 'low' reality not for any motives of social criticism but purely because of the stylistic stimulus given by the unconventional subject matter; this ambiguity was characteristic of both musical and literary naturalism in the late nineteenth century. The contemporaneity of the naturalism of Emile Zola and the exoticism of Pierre Loti in the novel, for example, can be regarded, from the standpoint of the history of ideas, as hardly fortuitous. Thirdly, even Zola can be observed transferring the burden of dramatic motivation from a socially determined environment to 'general human' feelings – that is, from something concrete and rational to something abstract and emotional – as soon as he put aside the novel and turned to writing opera librettos (for Alfred Bruneau). As librettist he conformed to the conditions imposed by the genre. This can be interpreted either as the triumph of operatic tradition or as a sign that naturalism must be measured in opera by some other yardstick than that which applies to the novel or the play. Fourthly, instead of being content to observe that Mascagni remained loyal to the traditions of the lyric theatre for long stretches of his score at a time, we should perhaps pay some attention to the complementary fact that, in contrast to Verdi's practice of continuing to compose in the cantabile style even when horrors are enacted on the stage, in Mascagni it is at the decisive moments of dramatic crisis and tragic catastrophe that the singing turns into speaking or screaming. Fifthly, the decision to integrate the on-stage music in *Cavalleria rusticana* stylistically, instead of attempting a montage or collage technique which would have led to stylistic fragmentation while allowing those numbers to stand out as instances of realism, was probably fortuitous and not dictated by a general principle enshrined in the aesthetics of veristic opera: there are scenes in other works (Act 1 of *Carmen*, Act 2 of *Bohème*) where the quotational – that is, realistic – nature of the on-stage music is thrown into high relief.

There is at least partial justification, therefore, for talking of verismo in opera; on the other hand, the refusal to engage in social criticism, the predominance, for long stretches, of the cantabile style of lyric theatre tradition, the avoidance of verbal and musical prose, and the indifference to quotation and montage as techniques for on-stage music are indubitably unrealist or antirealist traits which lay Mascagni and Puccini open to the charge of stylistic inconsistency. (But then, total consistency is one of the rarest conditions of artistic success.) It is nearer to the mark to think of nineteenth-century realism as an ideal type, constructed from a number of actual styles in varying proportions and offering realist features in different combinations rather than as something embodied, with all its attributes simultaneously on show, in certain specific works. Even as an ideal type, enabling us to see the connections between works which we would otherwise surely not relate to each other, realism is not a phantom but a historical fact.

9

Literature, history and 'history'

'After *Marriage*, the Rubicon is crossed . . . This is living prose in music', Modest Musorgsky wrote to Ludmila Shestakova in July 1868.[71] He was aware, therefore, of the significance of the experiment he was making, and equally aware of the risk attached to the idea of setting a prose text – an idea even Mily Balakirev thought was 'mad'.[72] And although Musorgsky broke off the composition of Nikolai Gogol's play *Marriage* after the first act, it does not mean that he regarded the experiment as a failure: dedicating the fragment to Vladimir Stasov in 1873, he called it a piece of himself. 'Compare it with *Boris*, bring 1868 and 1871 face to face, and you will see that I give you myself, irrevocably.'[73] Without *Marriage*, the earliest setting of a prose text in the history of opera, *Boris Godunov* would not have been written, and without *Boris* Debussy's *Pelléas et Mélisande* in turn is scarcely conceivable. So the experiment, even if it was not completed and the fragment has never been performed publicly, is part of what Walter Benjamin called 'the dawn of the history of the modern age'.

The idea of setting the text of a play word for word as it was written, without re-working it into a libretto in the usual way, came to Musorgsky from Alexander Dargomïzhsky, who started to compose Pushkin's *The Stone Guest* in 1866. It was Dargomïzhsky, too, who formulated the credo of Russian realism embraced so wholeheartedly by Musorgsky: 'I want the note to express the word, I want truth', he wrote in a letter in 1857, evidently inspired by Nikolai Chernïshevsky, whose manifesto *The Aesthetic Relationship of Art to Reality* (1855) provided the realism of Russian literature since Gogol with an aesthetic doctrine as well as quotable catchwords.

The precept that music ought to mirror the intonation and express the meaning of words is a commonplace which recurs perennially in the history of opera, whenever the cry goes up that the genre is corrupt and should be reformed. That it could gather the force of a dogma which actually changed the history of Russian music is astonishing, and at first hardly comprehensible to outsiders, because of all languages Russian is obviously one where the musical features of the spoken language are peculiarly well able to reproduce and represent both social character and individual, momentaneous, emotional reactions and states of mind.[74] But the decisive factor in the popularity which the idea of realism gained in Russian music seems to have been the recognition by Stasov, the aesthetic ideologist of the 'Mighty Handful', that the theory of realism offered an opportunity to be wholeheartedly modern and committedly nationalist at the same time. Stasov was a born publicist and, in the progressive atmosphere astir in Russia in the 1860s (Musorgsky, for one, had complied enthusiastically with the recent abolition of serfdom, though it nearly ruined him financially), he instinctively grasped that the doctrine of realism was a means firstly to place the music of Balakirev and his rebel circle on the same footing as the great Russian epic, secondly to demonstrate his, and their, modernity by appropriating the slogans of French art and literature criticism of the 1850s, and thirdly to assert their independence both of Italian opera, which the general public preferred, and of Wagnerian music drama, whose declared intentions were beginning to disturb the intelligentsia. In the name of the aesthetics of the true, as formulated by Dargomïzhsky, Stasov, who was a genius of negation, denounced both *opera seria*, in which the reality of emotion, he believed, was dissipated in the abstract cantabile lyricism of closed vocal numbers, and Wagnerian music drama, the mythological subject matter of which he regarded as an 'unnatural', absurd agglomeration of 'hallucinations and monstrous exaggerations'.

Dargomïzhsky's decision to set the text of *The Stone Guest* 'just as it is, without changing a single word' was of great significance, for it meant the repudiation of the formal framework of traditional opera, built up of recitatives, arias and ensembles. Nevertheless, it is a text written in blank verse, and there is a world of difference between that and the prose which Musorgsky undertook to set in *Marriage* – and later in some passages in *Boris*.

There are both technical and ideological aspects to the principle of musical prose, which is one of the central categories of realism. Technically it meant nothing less than the dismantling of traditional periodic structure – the essential factor of rhythmic organization over large spans, and thus the basis of cantabile vocal melody and of the impression of formal integration alike. Complementarity or correspondence – the principle that at each stage in the construction of a syntactical system every antecedent element is followed by a consequent element which counterbalances and completes it: bar corresponds to bar, phrase to phrase, clause to clause, period to period – was made irrelevant by the process of joining together elements of irregular length which corresponded to the elements of meaning in a prose text, without any regard for the metrical-cum-syntactical stereotype which the lay public believed to be an inherent part of the nature of music.

The result of the abandonment of traditional syntax, in the service of realism, was a difficult and delicate problem of form that a composer could not ignore even if, like Musorgsky, he held a view of realism that was antiformalist. If he started with the maxim that musical prose could guarantee an expression of feeling that was immediate, truthful, not distorted by stylization, and even capable of rendering the individual elements of an emotion, the composer had a choice of several paths by which to avoid the regression into an amorphousness which was the principal danger with musical prose. One possibility was to assert the presence of a metrical framework behind the surface irregularity of the individual vocal phrases whose length was dictated by the principle of expression rather than symmetry. This metrical framework was created by the totality of the vocal and instrumental phrase structures, and it gave the impression of at least a latent rhythmic organization over a large span. An alternative possibility was to trust in the dramaturgical strengths of 'dialogisierte Melodie': the adaptation of melodic writing to the confrontations characteristic of climaxes and turning points in spoken drama, creating a dramatic impact which was not destroyed by 'translation' into musical terms. A style of composition which could accommodate a structure built up of brief verbal exchanges benefited from the inner cohesion of the verbal model, and did not need to fall back on metrical correspondence and motivic associations. A third possibility, exemplified by Wagner's music dramas, was to create connections between metrically irregular, and therefore syntactically footloose, vocal phrases by the recurrence of motives of reminiscence or Leitmotive, whereby the orchestral writing becomes a network of thematic and motivic threads. Certainly the anti-Wagnerianism proclaimed by Stasov did not stop Musorgsky making extensive use of leitmotivic technique in *Boris*, which shows that he was more acutely aware of the formal problem in practice than he might admit in aesthetic theory.

None of these three methods of preventing musical prose from foundering in formlessness is, in any strict sense, realist. But in so far as they are among the conditions under which realism in opera appears feasible without succumbing to the formlessness risked by setting a text 'just as it is', a discussion of realism which omitted to consider structural procedures would be abstract in the worst sense.

It is understandable that some music historians have reservations about calling Musorgsky a musical realist without qualifying the term,[75] for although realism has been defined to the satisfaction of the historian of ideas,[76] that is not the case in the history of music, which is where Musorgsky ultimately belongs. Since Stasov, it has been a commonplace to mention Musorgsky's consciousness of an affinity between himself and the movements proclaimed as realism in Russian literature and painting, but there has never been a sufficiently exact definition of realism in terms of musical techniques and procedures (and Musorgsky himself apparently never used the word).

Musorgsky's position in the history of stylistic 'isms' is a paradoxical one. The age of positivism which dawned around the mid-century – after the failure of the revolution of 1848–9 and the decline of Hegelianism – remained an age of romanticism, or neo-romanticism, in music, which was thus out of step with the Zeitgeist. However extreme the contrast between Wagner and Liszt on the one hand and Brahms on the other may have seemed to their contemporaries, it was generally accepted, and said, that composers as a class, notwithstanding the partisan warfare between conservatives and progressives, were 'romantic' artists.

But if the neo-romanticism of the second half of the nineteenth century was a dominant trend in music and at odds with the Zeitgeist, the realism of Musorgsky was exactly the opposite: it was in step with the dominant tendency in the literature and painting of the age and at odds with music, which as a whole – in spite of Verdi and Bizet, Janáček and Charpentier – resisted the inroads of realism. If we are to find an explanation for this, we should first take seriously for once the nineteenth century's own thesis that music is 'of its nature' a romantic and unrealist art, whose proper sphere is the realm of the 'marvellous' – E. T. A. Hoffmann's Djinnistan or Atlantis – and not the 'prose of common life'. And if it is assumed that realism has no proper place in music, that it has only been imposed on music from outside to suit some aesthetic purpose and to some extent contradicts the very conditions of composition, then the charge of dilettantism which both contemporaries and later historians have brought against Musorgsky appears in a different light. Instead of being merely awkwardness and an accident of biography, the dilettantism begins to look like the price a musical realist had to pay for forcing on music a stylistic tendency which is alien to its nature. This can be expressed in another way: the phenomena that academic theorists regard as the signs of dilettantism may be – in the eyes of history – nothing other than the traces left on the music by musical realism, because of the degree of force used to impose it. The aesthetic weakness may be the reverse face of the historical authenticity – which is necessitated by the overall tendency of the age. But if we are prepared to grant a minimum amount of historical justification even to realism in music, as it is found in Musorgsky, then we cannot just dismiss the compositional consequences of the realist intention as dilettantism: we must take them seriously and without prejudice as artistic processes, and disregard any biographical or psychological considerations. It will then emerge that an interpretation of Musorgsky's irregularities, his rule-breaking, can be made on the basis of the same aesthetic categories as have been applied in modern literary theory to the style of the Russian realists – to the prose of Gogol and Tolstoy.

In Act 1 of *Boris Godunov*, in the scene in Pimen's cell, the novice Grigory recounts a dream which starts with him climbing the stairs of a frighteningly tall tower. Musically, the narration begins (Fig. 15) with a series of chords depicting the vertiginous climb with chromatic harmonies, the tonality of which could be described as 'floating', in Schoenberg's expression. The progression is formed from four major chords (E–C♯–A–F♯) which are repeated sequentially a whole tone higher, except that, in the repeat, the third chord is a semitone higher again than it should be (G♭–E♭–C–A♭, where regularity demands C♭ instead of C). If we temporarily ignore the presence of that third chord, we are left with an imperfect cadence of astonishing simplicity as the basic material to be repeated: I–(V)–II. To disrupt such a simple phrase with a conspicuous interpolation is certainly a conscious, considered act, not a naive one. The passage owes its expressive and symbolic effect, the realism of its depiction of Grigory's nightmare climb, to the impression of 'floating tonality', and that is entirely due to the waywardness of the interpolated chord. An effect like that is not the lucky result of the 'limited technical means and "awkward writing"' of which Stravinsky accuses Musorgsky:[77] it betrays a calculation which may be unusual, but whose steps can be traced.

Here is a second example from the same scene of *Boris*: the off-stage chorus of monks chanting a prayer (Fig. 9) uses harmonies which convey the effect of a church mode, in other words provide some musical local colour, or what Marxist aesthetic theorists would call 'milieu realism'. The last chord, C♯ minor in the sixth bar from Fig. 9, is simply inexplicable in terms of the rules of tonality as they were understood in the nineteenth century, except as the blunder of a dilettante. The progression V–II! in A major takes the place of a cadence, without performing its function, according to the criteria of major–minor tonality. But the archaicizing modality is also somewhat problematical as an instance of stylistic imitation: it is certainly not a case of simple reproduction of church-mode harmony as originally understood. While a 'Dorian' Sixth was just one degree among others in the sixteenth century, by the nineteenth it was recognized as a deviation from the minor scale and the 'characteristic' degree of the Dorian mode: it was solely by a reference to the minor scale, which the sixteenth century did not make but the nineteenth could not help making, that the concept of the 'Dorian' Sixth existed, as it had not in the sixteenth century. The alterations to which modal harmony was subjected in the nineteenth century were, so to speak, 'composed out' by Musorgsky. The conspicuously modal final chord, C♯ minor, is the unexpected conclusion of a chord progression, B minor – E major, which raises expectations of a tonal continuation and indeed was continued tonally earlier, in the choir's first lines (B major – E major – A major = II–V–I). The juxtaposition of a tonal and a modal version of the progression means nothing less, however, than that the C♯ minor chord, the modal element, is there because the composer deliberately decided against a tonal cadence, and his avoidance of the expected cadence is plain for all to see. The modality – the means whereby the realist, historical local colour was achieved, should therefore not be interpreted as a naivety; it must have been chosen by Musorgsky as a precisely calculated deviation from the tonal norm, and with full consciousness of the historical distance separating the nineteenth century from the sixteenth. Schoenberg would diagnose a lack of musical logic, because Musorgsky did not, at the end of the chorus, draw the musical consequences implicit in its start, but side-stepped into the unexpected. But this apparent sign of clumsiness is in fact a skilful device intended to create not only modal harmony but also the impression of the exotic, and thus to make the historical element of 'milieu realism' tangible. Musorgsky was a self-taught composer, but he was also undoubtedly an intellectual one.

The examination of Musorgsky's rule-breaking ought perhaps to go further than establishing where he departs from compositional norms in order to illustrate the text and represent the situation; an attempt should also be made to define the realism of those departures more precisely in its historical context as well as its significance for the history of ideas. A useful starting point for such an approach is an aesthetic theory long established in literary criticism under the name of 'Russian formalism'. The fact that an unbridgeable gulf exists for Marxists between the realism they proclaim and the formalism they deplore has not prevented Viktor Šklovskij from developing the argument that formalism is the aesthetic theory of the realist narrative technique of Gogol and Tolstoy.[78] As an intellectual discipline formalism is, in part at least, a theory of the artistic practice of realism.

The concept of alienation, a central category of formalist aesthetics made famous by Brecht, is interpreted by Šklovskij to mean that the goal of realist art is to revive attentiveness towards objects and circumstances, the perception of which has become stereotyped, and to do so by applying the irritant of an artistic technique which has not been dulled by familiarity. The process is thus simultaneously realist and formalist: realist, because it makes it possible to experience a segment of reality which has become unrecognizable as the response to it has become automatic; formalist, because it exploits the artifice of art to revive and stimulate perceptions which have grown dull and stereotyped – in other words, by disrupting conventions and schematized practices to some extent, it recreates the power of fresh, original perception.

Brief though they were, the analyses of two examples of Musorgsky's musical realism should have made sufficiently clear that it disturbs and disrupts conventional listening practices and stereotyped responses to music. Musorgsky was certainly the most decided despiser of convention in the nineteenth century. He was as sceptical towards the style of Italian opera, which pressed melody into predictable rhythmic moulds, determined by a very restricted number of verse metres, as he was towards German symphonic style, whose thematic-motivic working he regarded as mechanical and pedantic. He turned his back resolutely on what was considered to be 'musical logic', and scorned to develop thematic ideas on the Beethovenian model, to modulate as a means of mediating between remote tonalities, or to fill out melodic ideas to make eight-bar periods. Instead, rebelling against all the rules of his trade, as they were understood by 'good musicians', he set one motive up in opposition to another, allowed contrasting keys to clash together without any form of transition, and dissolved regular periodic construction in musical prose – all of which can be interpreted, without exaggeration or misrepresentation, as 'alienation' in Šklovskij's sense: the formalist exploitation of artistic techniques in the pursuit of realism.

The process of illustrating the text and representing situations musically by the use of unconventional and hence attention-rousing techniques, though drastic, is not in itself sufficient grounds for terming Musorgsky's style musical realism. It is only in combination with other factors that the elements which lend themselves to formalist interpretation come to constitute the phenomenon, or complex of phenomena, which the historian recognizes as nineteenth-century realism. As demonstrated in an earlier chapter, a concept of realism which is relevant specifically to the history of the arts and intends to avoid the epistemological trap – the labyrinthine debate as to what reality, or true reality, is – can adopt as its starting point the simple historical fact that nineteenth-century realism came into existence as an expression of rebellion against idealism, classicism and romanticism.

The choice of subject matter in nineteenth-century realist art (a rough-and-ready criterion, but not to be dismissed out of hand, as has been said) was characterized on the one hand by the avoidance of mythology and fairy tale in favour of the mundane, of intersubjective (publicly observable) reality, and, on the other hand, by a liking for subjects and situations which had previously been considered unsuitable for artistic treatment. As a polemical argument, reproaching realism for preferring ugly and unsavoury subjects (whether for reasons of aesthetics or social criticism) did not get very far; yet the fact remains that the element of challenge, of subversion, in realism is what struck opponents with the greatest force.

Over and above that, the concept of realism in association with the history of the arts needs to be qualified by reference to the aesthetic norms of each genre. As Erich Auerbach demonstrated in his book *Mimesis*, realism developed by a process of deliberately breaking the classical rule of stylistic differentiation between social classes which continued to influence the theory of the arts until the nineteenth century. According to that rule as it was applied to drama, including opera, tragedy and an elevated style were reserved for personages of noble blood and high rank, while the bourgeois and the peasant could be represented in the theatre only in comedy and therefore in a 'low' style. In so far as the lower classes came under the gaze of art at all, it was only from the perspective of their social superiors, that is, as objects of amusement. (Thus the emancipation of the bourgeoisie in literature was proclaimed not in comedy but in middle-class tragedy.)

If therefore, as has often been stated, the true hero of *Boris* is the Russian people, to a more pronounced degree in the opera than in Pushkin's play, the particular aspect of realism represented by the rule of stylistic class distinctions lies not so much in the mere presence of the crowd on the stage as in the fact that the crowd is the protagonist of a tragedy, and not of a comedy. The Russian people, as the collective subject of the drama, is invested with the dignity of tragedy, and that dignity also extends to individuals such as the Simpleton, who is not a grotesque but a touching figure. Conversely, the literary precedents of the domestic interlude when the tsar is seen with his children and their nurse have to be sought in the tradition of *comédie larmoyante*, and the idyll constitutes a drastic descent from the elevated style which a subject like the life of Boris should maintain, according to classicist rules.

Another postulate of realism is that art should concern itself with contemporary subjects; the fact that the subject of *Boris* is a historical one seems to be at odds with this, suggesting that either the theory needs to be revised or the categorization of the opera as realist should be reconsidered. Indeed, there is a dichotomy between the dogma that realist art must have a setting in the present or the immediate past and the historical fact that some of the essential criteria of realist art were developed in the nineteenth-century historical novel, including the insertion of 'petits détails vrais' in a fictional narrative, the use of local colour, and above all the depiction of the circumstances from which the action of the novel springs as a panorama of society, revealing the social mechanisms which influence the events in the narrative. (In *Les chouans*, Balzac was still imitating Scott and, technically, his later novels of social life still have something of the historical novel about them, in spite of their contemporary settings.) The dichotomy becomes less significant if we accept that the essential, decisive factor is not the setting of a work in the present or the past, but rather the assignment of a positive role to history: events and circumstances should be shown as conditioned by history and capable of being different had history been different, and not as dependent solely on the workings of timeless, universal human nature. The concept of 'historicity' has to do less with the period in which a narrative is set than with the manner of the narration; if the latter is informed by a sense of history as a totality of social processes in which the events narrated have a natural place, then it has earned the epithet 'realist', regardless of whether the time of the events is the present or the past.

It would seem, then, that there is no reason to exclude *Boris* from the category of realist art simply on the grounds that it belongs to a genre which can loosely be called 'historical'. On the other hand, if the opera as a whole and not the libretto alone is to be designated 'realist', it has to be shown convincingly that there is a close and necessary functional connection between the specifically musical dramaturgy of the work and the characteristics which distinguish *Boris* from other operas with historical subjects. *Boris* is a 'history' in the Shakespearean sense, and the difference is great enough to amount to the distinction of two separate operatic genres. This is most tellingly demonstrated if *Boris* is compared, not with an *opera seria* in which history has been nothing more than a source of material for the libretto, but with one of those operas by Meyerbeer which even highly critical contemporaries like Peter Cornelius and Heinrich Heine praised for the physically tangible presence in them of the spirit of history.

In *Le prophète*, Meyerbeer and Scribe wrote a tragedy which centres on the Anabaptist sect in the Low Countries in the sixteenth century. It differs from the countless operas with historical settings composed in the seventeenth and eighteenth centuries, in that the crowd plays a visible dramatic role in it as activator – or victim – of political events, instead of either being completely absent from the scene or at best providing supernumeraries. History is shown as a process of social interaction and change, and not in the passive function of a repository of intrigues which can be ransacked for excuses for the expression of a well-contrasted range of personal emotions.

In at least one respect, however, *Le prophète* resembles a conventional *opera seria* rather closely: its plot depends on a fictional private situation, acted out by soloists in bel canto, and the public political events which bring the crowd on to the stage in huge musical and scenic set-pieces are represented as the consequences of that private, personal action. And the inner divisions of the material, the oscillation between private intrigue and public historical process as the driving force of the drama, is exactly correlative to a musical dramaturgy which on the one hand indulges a penchant for the overwhelming effect of packing the stage, in scenes for chorus and ensembles, with all the musical and theatrical resources of the grandest of grand opera, and on the other hand makes no attempt to relinquish the stock forms of *opera seria* – aria, cavatina and duet. (More an inheritor than an innovator, Meyerbeer never moved remotely near to 'musical prose' or 'dialogisierte Melodie' in either Wagner's or Musorgsky's sense.)

Meyerbeer's conception of historical drama differs, therefore, from the Shakespearean history, of which *Boris* is the prime operatic example, firstly in its retention of closed musical forms in contrast to the formal freedom which Musorgsky had from

Pushkin and Pushkin from Shakespeare, and secondly in its
fidelity to operatic tradition in making a private intrigue the true
motive for the outwardly political action. The conflicting claims
of might and right, the mechanisms of expedience and *force
majeure* which drive the wheels of the struggle for power in
Shakespeare's histories, are depicted in *Le prophète* as the outcome of emotional conflicts in which politics originally had no
part at all.

And yet the opera dates from an age when the masses were a
force in politics, when people threw up barricades and fought for
their ideas in the streets. The representation of private concerns
as the motivation for political events looks at first like retro-
gression into an antiquated mode of thought, dating from the age
of absolutism, apart from the somewhat token gesture that some
of the principals are bourgeois rather than noble. When, in Act
3 of *Le prophète*, John decides to storm Münster, not for the
good military reason that the Anabaptists are under threat from
the imperial army, but because he has had news of Bertha's flight
to the city, it almost seems like a caricature of conventional
operatic motivation. It is a totally inappropriate assertion of a
private interest as grounds for undertaking a serious political and
historical action, in which the spirit of opera – and indirectly the
spirit of the age of absolutism in which opera grew up – triumphs
over the realities of history. However, the mingling of politics
and private concerns in *Le prophète* is not only a matter of formal
conservatism – the fact that the work is still a 'number opera';
there is also an aspect of personal conservatism which obviously
had a profound influence on the dramatic structure of the work.
It can be stated without exaggeration that all the political groups
represented in *Le prophète* are painted in the blackest possible
colours: the aristocracy is brutal and tyrannical, the leaders of the
Anabaptists are corrupt, hypocritical and advocates of violence,
and the citizens of Münster are the cowardly, oppressed, pusil-
lanimous victims of history, which rolls over them like fate. In
other words, Meyerbeer has taken sides, not as regards the political issues of his opera, but against politics altogether. Politics is
shown to be the epitome of wrong and the source of misfortune,
and it is set off against the idyll from which John, Bertha and
Fidès are snatched by force. Meyerbeer's, and Scribe's, grand
opera is a political opera born from an unpolitical spirit.

All the same, the significance of this personal attitude
should not be allowed to overshadow the greater importance of

the formal basis of Meyerbeer's dramaturgy. Meyerbeer, unlike Musorgsky, was not interested in the 'history' (in the Shakespearean sense) as a dramatic genre, or in the problems of realizing that concept in the musical theatre. His field was the genre of grand opera, where there were formal requirements which, on this occasion, he sought to satisfy with a historical subject, while at other times he would take romantic subjects (as in *Robert le diable*). At the stylistic stage which the genre had reached in the 1830s and 1840s, a grand opera simply could not have been written without the plot framework of private relationships manifested in arias, cavatinas and romanzas, duets and ensembles. But though the motivation of political events by private intrigue was thus a matter of formal necessity, grand opera was also capable of representing a mass of people in the grip of politically aroused emotions with a scenic power which the spoken theatre could not rival. Crowd scenes can be an embarrassment to the director in the spoken theatre, but in grand opera, if the 'number' structure is the skeleton, the crowd scene is the spinal column. The social consequences of politics, therefore, in so far as they are of the essence of the 'history' genre – and they are indeed part of the substance of all historical drama – could be represented scenically in opera, apparently the least 'realist' theatrical medium, with an ease and conviction which went far beyond anything the non-musical theatre could manage at that date.

Whereas *Le prophète* is marked, as a historical drama, by an ambivalence, the political implications of which can be interpreted as a consequence of the musical dramaturgy, while its musico-dramaturgical structure can be interpreted, conversely, as the outward sign and expression of a political philosophy, *Boris Godunov*, by contrast, is a 'history', or 'chronicle play' in the terminology of Shakespearean criticism, presented through the medium of music, and it is the first and only example of the genre in the entire history of music to exemplify the Shakespearean genre. Clearly, there were no precedents in musical drama on which Musorgsky could model his attempt to realize the Shakespearean prototype in operatic form, and it is equally obvious that the central problems to which the work offers a solution are closely intertwined with the literary tradition confronting Pushkin when he undertook to represent Russian history in the spirit of Shakespeare. Where the dramaturgical structure of Meyerbeer's opera rests on existing musical forms, that of

Musorgsky's opera is the response to the formal conditions imposed by his choice of a historical subject.

Boris Godunov, like the tragedies of the theatre of the age in which it is set, is about the isolation, the fears and the despair experienced by someone who has risen to absolute power. Politics is presented as it is in Shakespeare's plays, as Jan Kott has pointed out, in the form of a doomed cycle of distrust and acts of violence. The sense of guilt for the death of the tsarevich, by which Boris is weighed down, is like a prison from which he cannot escape; and he is ensnared in the dialectical and tragic irony that his attempt to purge his guilt by ruling as a rational modern monarch leads inevitably to further disaster and ultimately fails altogether because of the irrationality of the ruled. The Russian people are incapable of responding to the voice of reason, are easily swayed by superstitious apprehensions and rumour, and fall victim in the end to the deceit of a usurper. The isolation in which Boris is immured is represented dramaturgically by the structural use of monologue as the medium for the inner action. His address in the Coronation scene, which stands out conspicuously in the context of the ritual surrounding it, the aria in Act 2 which, though ostensibly directed to his son, is really a soliloquy delivered in the presence of witnesses, as well as the scene of his madness and death in the last act, are all monologues, formally speaking; and their effect as expressions of loneliness is all the greater for the fact that Boris is not, to the eye, alone at all. The use of monologue is far more extreme in Musorgsky's opera than in Pushkin's play, in which the monologues take the form of interpolations in extended scenes of dialogue expounding the intrigues of the nobility at Boris's court. There is some truth in the argument that the change in emphasis is a matter of the craft of libretto-making, but it falls short of providing a complete explanation; undoubtedly the concentration on monologue at the expense of the dialogues in which political – that is, public – intrigue is conducted has a foundation in the nature of opera, but at the same time it brings out one of the major themes of the Shakespearean history and of baroque tragedy: the isolation and despair of the ruler are presented through the medium of the musical theatre with an immediacy and vividness beyond the capabilities of the spoken theatre.

Another factor which receives greater emphasis in the opera than in Pushkin's play is the relationship between Boris and the Russian people; it is not entirely absent from the play, but its greater prominence in the opera is in part complementary to the structural role of the monologues. In the opera the crowd is more truly the antagonist than the usurper Grigory, for the tragedy of Boris is that his desire to rule rationally and even benevolently is perverted when the ruled prove irrational. The opera ends differently from the play, with the scene in the Kromy forest, showing the people in a state of anarchy which is dramatically an exact counterpart to the madness of the tsar. The difference in the way the two works end is no accident: Musorgsky was able to exploit the specific advantage which the large crowd scene, the massed tableau for chorus and ensemble – the spinal column of Meyerbeerian grand opera – gives opera over the spoken drama. And if the scenes in Pushkin in which the nobles hatch their plots are reduced to a few remnants in Musorgsky's libretto, the crowd scenes, which could be no more than rudimentary in Pushkin, are the more dominant by contrast. But even if Musorgsky seized the opportunities offered him by the nature of musical drama, he was by no means guilty of forcing his historical subject into the straitjacket of an existing musical form. Far from it: like the structural role of the monologues, the emphasis on the crowd scenes developed out of the substance of the action, which consists in the tragic dialectics of the relationship of ruler and ruled. It is no exaggeration to claim a place for Musorgsky's libretto in literary history, too: its contribution to the study of the influence of Pushkin's drama – understood as an exploration of the structures of the 'history' genre – is to demonstrate that the other face of the drama of isolation is the drama of the people.

Boris Godunov thus combines a compositional technique which is realist (according to the criteria of the aesthetics of the true) in its use of musical prose, its adaptation of melody to dramatic dialogue, and its expressivity based on the intonations of speech, with a musical dramaturgy which also fulfils one of the postulates of realism (as the dominant aesthetic doctrine of the later nineteenth century) in its exposition of an episode of history in terms that are 'historical' in the positive sense, placing the episode in a social process. The tragic dialectics working itself out between the tsar immured in the monologues and the people whose anarchy erupts in the crowd scenes is fundamentally different from the relationship presented in *Le prophète*, between a private action which provides the framework for a 'number' opera, and the public, political consequences which are drawn from it in large choral scenes. The difference, indeed, is as fundamental as that between the authentic historical dialectics of the one work (which is therefore realist because it is authentic) and the pseudo-causality which, in a drama ostensibly about a mass movement, exemplifies the doctrine, implanted in *opera seria* by the political realities of the age of absolutism, that politics merely reflects the private affairs of those who think they are the makers of history.

10

The 'musical novel'

In October 1866 Georges Bizet wrote in a letter: 'More realism, a *juste milieu* is not for me.'[79] By '*juste milieu*' he meant the style of Meyerbeer, forged in the 1830s. The realism to which he declared his allegiance here, ten years after Champfleury's manifesto and ten years before the first performance of *Carmen*, was a stylistic principle which postulated a coherent functional relationship between the elements of subject matter, dramaturgical structure, aesthetic principles and musical means. In his realization of that relationship Bizet demonstrated that opera was capable of a depiction of reality which, for inner logic, conceded nothing to realism in literature or the visual arts.

But although music historians appear to be in complete agreement in bestowing the epithet 'realist' on Bizet – he, Musorgsky and Janáček are the only three composers whose right to it has never been questioned – there is a great divergence of opinion when it comes down to stating the terms of reference or defining the characteristics which justify the description of *Carmen* as a realist opera. Having adopted the term from the history of literature and the visual arts, music historians have used it with an uncertainty, at the heart of which is the feeling that music – that of the nineteenth century at any rate – is 'really' a romantic art.

Paul Bekker spoke of 'melodic realism', a term he did not analyse but by which he meant the impassioned cantabile style originating with Verdi, and he apostrophized Verdi as the first 'musical realist'. But if, like Bekker, one is merely seeking an antonym for 'bel canto', the function is performed quite adequately by 'descriptive' (which there is no justification for narrowing down to 'realist'). In any case, Bizet's realism is only one factor in Bekker's exposition; in the same context, as if Bizet was an eclectic who sampled every stylistic trend of the second half of the nineteenth century, Bekker speaks of 'psychologism' on account of the gestural, expressive nature of the orchestration, and of romanticism on account of the exotic subject matter, piling up the concepts as only a popularizer can:

Bizet was as much subject to psychologism as Wagner was, as the motivic elaboration of his score shows. He was as much a melodic realist as Verdi, as his subordination of the melodic line to the expression of emotion shows. He was as much a romantic as either of them, as his use of Spanish colour shows, especially in the instrumentation.[80]

Donald Jay Grout, on the other hand, identified realism as the characteristic style of *Carmen* as a whole, but was too conscious of the historical limitations of the trend to speak of a musical age of realism, represented by this opera. Without mentioning the Meyerbeerian type of historical grand opera at all, Grout emphasized the importance of the difference between the subject matter of *Carmen* and those of *drame lyrique* and mythological music drama: 'Bizet's rejection of a sentimental or mythological plot was significant of a narrow but important anti-Romantic movement toward realism in late nineteenth-century opera.'[81]

If choosing a subject set in the present time and in a milieu which would cause offence to some was a bold stroke of realism in writing an opera, it was an area of realism where *La traviata* had already shown the way: Verdi had also provided a model for the 'realism of expression' which Paul Bekker referred to without describing adequately; both these characteristics of *Carmen* are among the constituents of the musical realism of the nineteenth century, and there is a third in the 'stylistic mixture' which Walter Niemann felt to be so prominent a feature of the work. (They are all also among the categories of realism which music shared with literature and painting.) Evidently without being conscious of the historical preconceptions of his observation, or of its significance in terms of art history, Niemann spoke of 'a remarkably vacillating sense of style, which is no more shy of tragedy than of operetta in its unique mixture of tragic passion, veristic realism and uproarious humour'.[82]

The possibility that Bizet broke the old rule of stylistic class distinction consciously and calculatedly in order to carry out an aesthetic programme of operatic realism is at best highly remote and can probably be ruled out altogether. It is therefore all the more remarkable and significant that his stylistic instinct prompted him to give form to a principle which even writers in the fields of literature and the visual arts (like Gautier in the polemic against Courbet quoted in an earlier chapter and in a different context) were still having difficulty in formulating.

Carmen is a tragedy. (Its official description as '*opéra comique*' is due to the spoken dialogue of the original version.) But it is a tragedy which breaks with the classicist norm by taking place in a milieu that a Marxist would identify as that of the 'Lumpenproletariat'. The middle-class tragedy which was the earliest form of protest against the assumptions of aristocratic tragedy was still hardly established in opera, when *Carmen* replaced it with a plebeian tragedy (and in a form, moreover, which recalls the novels of the Goncourt brothers in the impossibility of separating the strand of social subversiveness from the aestheticist pleasure in unfamiliar stimuli, to which Nietzsche reacted so vehemently.)

It is not the social milieu of *Carmen* as such, however, which is the decisively realist factor; as Walter Niemann recognized, it is the opportunity the milieu provides for a plausible and abrupt move from operetta to tragedy: the tragedy is all the more moving because it does not overshadow the whole opera but emerges swiftly from ambush, as it were, to break over the characters' heads.

The work is a tragedy not simply because of its outcome, but because both Carmen and Don José, with a courage born of despair, shoulder a destiny which both secretly know will allow them no escape. Although there is not a single duet in the work in which the pair express unanimity of emotion, there is between them the latent mutual understanding of the condemned, growing out of the dark awareness of an inescapable joint destiny in which each is the victim of the other.

Walter Felsenstein's maxim that there must be a 'foundation' or 'motive' for the music in an opera has come to be adopted as the cornerstone of realist music theatre, yet at first acquaintance it sounds curiously 'anti-operatic', because it contradicts the deeply rooted belief that the music in opera represents an expressive convention which has to be accepted, while it is as futile as it is superfluous to try to justify it with reflections on the 'character of the reality' of music. (If the convention is not accepted, opera turns unexpectedly into parody for the disinterested observer.) But *Carmen*, of all operas, shows that Felsenstein's criteria are completely valid within certain well-defined limits. The fact that they apply only to one, historically circumscribed style, instead of possessing a universal currency, is an advantage rather than a drawback for a historian whose concern is not with musical realism, or realism in the musical theatre, as a whole, but specifically with that of the nineteenth century. Although realism, as Felsenstein understood it and practised it, is far from representing a general norm for operatic dramaturgy, the principles on which he based it are very illuminating in the case of certain works of the late nineteenth and early twentieth centuries.

The fact that *Carmen*, in its original version, is '*opéra comique*' with spoken dialogue should not be dismissed as a fortuitous nod in the direction of Parisian theatrical convention; it has to be taken seriously, as an aesthetic precondition which Bizet accepted with his eyes open. There is undoubtedly a connection between the premiss that the music in an *opéra comique*, burgeoning as it does out of spoken dialogue, must have a motive instead of being merely a 'given' circumstance and the fact that *Carmen* is exceptionally well endowed with musical numbers which are to some extent 'real' music, which is being 'quoted' on the stage; in the first act alone, the street urchins' march, the Habañera and Carmen's Chanson are all 'on-stage music'. But the process of including fragments of musical reality – or musically stylized fragments of acoustic reality – in an opera has always beeen regarded and hailed as 'realist': spoken dialogue and 'real' music, which would also stand in a spoken play, are two aspects of the same thing.

The consequences which the montage-like technique has for the other numbers in the opera are even more significant. It might appear that the musical language is merely representative of the conventions of the genre, the numbers aesthetically self-sufficient and not requiring any motivation. Felsenstein, however, under the pressure of a realist philosophy, felt obliged to pursue his argument: and his maxim that a production must show the characters falling prey to passions which compel them to express themselves by singing rather than speaking is undoubtedly persuasive – but it does not tell the whole story. For

Felsenstein misunderstands, or fails even to see, the strange fact that the great impassioned duet in which contrary or concordant emotions are outpoured, and which forms the backbone of any opera by Verdi, is almost entirely absent from *Carmen*. There are numbers in which an unrestrained cantabile tone breaks through – the duet for Don José and Micaela (No. 6), the 'Flower Song' in the duet for Don José and Carmen (No. 16), Micaela's aria (No. 21), or parts of the finale duet (No. 26) – but in all of them the expressivity, for all its urgency, is directed to some extent into a void: dramatically and musically, it evokes no response. Yet it is precisely the hopelessness of the emotion with which Micaela confronts Don José, and he Carmen, which gives the opera its tragic undertow. And the fact that an emotion which in reality would probably remain unspoken, or at best be stammered out, takes the form of a cantilena in opera is emphatically not 'unrealistic'. Music in these circumstances becomes 'sounding silence', as Wagner put it, and no further dramaturgical foundation is needed. A passion which is to some extent thrown back on itself, every bit as much as the eruptive passions which demand gestural musical expressions on Felsenstein's terms, is an immediately intelligible dramatic motive for music when, as in *opéra comique*, it is not the only means of expression to hand.

If conducting dialogue in melody is a stylistic principle of musical theatre to which drama requires reality to bend, one of the realistic traits of Bizet's opera which defies that principle is the fact that the essential tragedy of Don José and Carmen takes place almost wordlessly, in the breaks between the numbers of 'on-stage' music. The Chanson in No. 9, and the Dance Song and Tarantella in No. 16 are 'real' music; on the other hand Don José's urgently expressive cantabile (Nos 16 and 26) receives no response, except in the form of Carmen's mocking parody (No. 16). On the few occasions when they do engage in direct exchanges of dialogue the music falls back into accompanied recitative (Nos 9, 16 and 26).

The difference from Verdi is thus almost as great as the difference from Wagner. *Carmen* offers neither the impassioned duet, in which emotions burst upon each other in the stylized forms of cantabile or cabaletta, nor the reasoned exposition of a dialogue which lays bare the implications of an emotional situation; the medium of Bizet's drama is the scene, assembled from musically heterogeneous items, and, as Walter Niemann observed, the lack of homogeneity is an expression of the tragic alienation between the protagonists who, indissolubly bound together as they are, cannot talk to each other. All the music in *Carmen* – the 'on-stage' numbers, the expressions of despair to which there is no response, the stammered outbursts which meet with mockery – revolves around the dark centre where there are no words and where the tragedy of Carmen and Don José is really acted out.

Bizet was able to preserve a distance from his work which recalls Gustave Flaubert's 'impassibilité'; Nietzsche admired it as 'aristocratic'. Artists who were inspired by *Carmen* on the one hand and the novels of Zola on the other to write veristic or naturalistic operas in the 1890s either did not recognize this or at any rate seldom respected it. Instead they ran riot with the conventions of the lyric theatre and of Tonmalerei. Certainly a self-confessed musical naturalist like Alfred Bruneau (who set librettos by Zola) meant the crudest kind of tone painting when he spoke of 'realistic' music, as the antithesis, as Schumann might have said, of 'poetic' music.[83]

Yet the belief that the roots of French – and Italian – naturalism lay in *Carmen* was not without justification. Arthur Seidl was a Wagnerian and a German nationalist whose *parti pris* nevertheless helped him to more insight than is to be found in attempts to mete out evenhanded aesthetic justice. Seidl set out the differences between Wagner and Bizet in a chain of antitheses which amounts to nothing less than an entire theory of *fin de siècle* musical realism, allowing for a degree of polemical distortion.

In order to characterize more precisely the contrast (as we will call it) between Germanic art and Romance art, bearing in mind that the contrast is best summed up in Nietzsche's formula 'Wagner – Bizet', I will at this stage trace only some obvious lines of demarcation and draw certain parallels more closely. They are as follows: music drama – musical novel; three acts – five tableaux; free verse – unrestrained prose; measured prosody – arbitrary intonation; gods, heroes, kingship, knights – man, coffee house littérateur, labourer, seamstress; guilds of burghers – an artistic Bohemia; alfresco high art – impressionist daubing depicting a 'milieu' from a proletarian angle; aristocratic selection – egalitarianism; moral and aesthetic – social and technical; synthesis – analysis (in technical procedures); polyphony – homophony; the riot in *Die Meistersinger* – a strike by smiths or a demonstration by seamstresses; listening to the Forest Murmurs in the solitude of the primeval glade or hearing the morning fanfare amid the purity of nature – urban hubbub, sweltering summer heat and the brooding rumble of the world of commerce starting to life in the city with its vaporous stench and its sundry 'cries'.[84]

Obviously, besides *Carmen*, Seidl is referring to Gustave Charpentier's *Louise* and Puccini's *La Bohème*.

The source of the phrase 'musical novel' is the sub-title ('roman musical') of Charpentier's opera, and Seidl recognized that it referred to the dramaturgical structure of the work as well as to the dramatic importance of the urban setting; the division by 'tableaux' ['Bilder' – both 'scenes' and 'pictures'] rather than 'acts' is taken as the outward manifestation of an epic, 'open' form which has renounced the postulates of classicist dramatic theory. Instead of a close-knit structure of 'actions' which interlock in such a way as to bring about the tragic outcome, the 'musical novel' is formed from a loose-knit series of 'tableaux', and the 'milieu', instead of merely serving as a background to the action seen on the stage, advances to the footlights and plays a quasi-active role in the drama – or 'theatrical narrative'. Finally, the chief dramatic medium is, again, not so much the impassioned duet for principals as the picturesque ensemble, in which the individual characters figure as the staffage in a painting.

A conservative with a very precisely tuned instinct, Seidl recognized – and opposed – the peopling of the stage with littérateurs and workers in the place of gods and heroes for the act of social and aesthetic rebellion that it was intended to be in the realism of the nineteenth century (even though, as in the novels of the Goncourts, social criticism might be mixed with aesthetic motives). Seidl had no difficulty in seeing the element of sedition involved in the breaking of the old law of stylistic class distinction, as he implicitly reveals in his opposition of 'high art' to the 'proletarian angle'; and his reaction, expressed in the polemical 'egalitarianism', was political.

On the other hand he does not appear to have recognized that the shift of milieu from mythology to the big modern city was inseparable from the dramaturgical structure of the realist operas which he apostrophized as 'musical novels'. Essentially, the protagonist of *Louise* – and even of *La Bohème* – is not the 'heroine' whose sad fate the opera recounts but the city of Paris itself, to whom Charpentier and Puccini give a musical presence. The fact that a 'seamstress' becomes involved in a tragedy as if she was one of the aristocracy for whom Seidl would prefer to see tragedy reserved is one of the associated aspects of a dramaturgy in which the location – specifically the milieu of a large city – is not simply the 'setting' but one of the 'actors'. The sense that the city plays an active part in the events, in these operas as in Zola's novels, is

part of a process of mythologizing the city. In the street scenes in
Louise and *La Bohème*, the scenery is less a function of the cast
of human characters than the characters are a function of the
scenery. And this reversal of roles, whereby the depiction of a
milieu in 'tableaux' acquires more significance than the confrontation of human figures in 'acts', is the dramaturgical correlative
to the change of emphasis in staging techniques when a work is in
a 'free' form with a loose-knit structure instead of a tight-knit
'closed' form.

   In one respect Seidl's catalogue of the differences between
mythological music drama and realist opera comes close to an
apparently quite deliberate distortion of the facts, and that is in
the inclusion of a distinction between verse and prose. By purely
prosodic criteria the alliterative lines in which Wagner wrote the
text of the *Ring* (in order to present his Germanic subject matter
in a Germanic form) are verse, but it is a form of verse which
accommodates any number of accented syllables in a line, and
any number of unaccented syllables between the accents; the
result might as well be prose, for musical purposes. The outcome
of the attempt to find an appropriate musical form for alliterative
verse was 'musical prose': unconcerned with metrical rules of
complementarity, or correspondence, Wagner forged together
phrases of irregular length according to a structural principle
which was no longer – as it still was in *Lohengrin* – based on the
period of four- or eight-bar groups but on the network of leitmotivic technique.

   Accordingly, irrespective of stylistic differences between
music drama and realist opera, musical prose was the premiss
that the realist composers of the late nineteenth century had in
common with Wagner – much as Seidl laboured to deny it. From
the point of view of music history, the prose principle provided
the technical justification for the musical trend. Seidl had the
perspicacity to recognize the phenomenon, but his conservatism
made him distrust it. It is not even necessary to refer to Wagner's
latent affinity with realism – revealed when one recognizes the
physiognomy of a scene from Ibsen beneath the mythological
surface of the dialogues between Wotan and Fricka – in order to
recognize that musical prose is the technical correlative of the
dramaturgy of the musical novel.

11

Realistic melody
and dramaturgical construction

The hermeneutical maxim that historians and textual critics are not obliged to accept without question everything an author says about his own work, in other words, that it is not inevitably the case that the intentions which a work patently realizes correspond exactly to the intentions expressed by the work's creator when discussing it, is an incontestable ground rule. Interpreters are mistaken, however, in referring to the dubious competence of the author to pronounce on his own affairs as justification for disregarding awkward contradictions which hinder straightforward exegesis. They might do better to recognize in the apparently incomprehensible the traces of a problem which it may not be possible to solve completely but which, if reconstructed, may lead closer to the real historical life of a work than will a mere classification within a ready-made stylistic category.

The fact that Leoš Janáček expressed enthusiasm over Mascagni's *Cavalleria rusticana* in 1892, at the time immediately prior to the conception of *Jenůfa*, while his attitude to Musorgsky (whose *Boris*, admittedly, he did not study or comment on until 1909, after *Jenůfa* was finished) was evidently sceptical and reserved, has been a cause of confusion and perplexity to a school of criticism which looks for the connections and common ground in a given historical period. Such critics take the realist aspirations of Italian verismo less seriously, while being overwhelmed by verismo's lyric and theatrical energy; at the same time the connection between Musorgsky and Janáček seems obvious and indisputable, manifested as it is both in their common adherence to an aesthetics of the true and in their choosing to set prose texts in a melodic style which rests on the inflexions of speech. Janáček's expressed preference can, it seems, be interpreted only as a blind spot which defies any further explanation. If however we venture beyond mere description of style, in the form of enumeration of musical features, and reconstruct the underlying

95

compositional issue – style can be said to be like a text which is not understood until the question to which it is the answer has been identified – then Janáček's reserve towards Musorgsky can be examined in the light of its motivation.

Beset by the post-Wagnerian uncertainties of the 1890s, Janáček found reassurance in *Cavalleria rusticana* that his idea of musical realism was not just the provincial conception of a committed nationalist and folklorist but a significant international trend; at the same time Mascagni's stylistic concerns were so remote from Janáček's problems that he was free to acknowledge the virtues of verismo without selfconsciousness. On the other hand, when he first set eyes on the score of *Boris* in 1909, he discovered that, while he and Musorgsky undoubtedly served the same principles in matters of aesthetics and musical dramaturgy, the Russian had not even been aware of the existence of the fundamental technical problem that Janáček had faced in *Jenůfa*, let alone solved it.

Musorgsky's solution of the problem of how to develop a coherent and consistent musical fabric in opera from a melodic style based on speech inflexions was one which struck the composer of *Jenůfa*, in 1909, as 'Wagnerish': as representing a stage of evolution he had left behind him in the leitmotivic technique of *Šárka* (1887), and as failing to acknowledge what he saw to be the essential problem. Founded in the inflexions of speech, the vocal line should present a mosaic of 'snapshots of the soul', as Janáček put it; but Musorgsky's vocal line is supported by an orchestral line shaped by the use of Leitmotiv. The effect of leitmotivic technique, as a form-building principle, on a montage of momentary impressions is to subsume it into a synthetic structure: what Wagner called 'web' or 'weave' (Gewebe) in terms of its construction, while Thomas Mann described its aesthetic power as the 'sorcery of associations' (Beziehungszauber). Janáček perceived in Musorgsky a lack of consistency, in the discrepancy between a realist vocal line and a symbolic-cum-structural orchestral fabric; for his part Janáček persisted in the pursuit of his ideal of a wholly consistent interrelationship between the motivic style of vocal and orchestral writing – an amazing undertaking on the premiss of a melody determined by speech inflexions. The fact that 'speech melody', intended to meet the needs of musical truth, is essentially vocal, did not deter Janáček from transmuting it into instrumental idioms and orchestral material. (And that Musorgsky, between the two stools of vocal and instrumental idiom, did not even conceive of the question of their interrelationship as a problem, seems to be the grounds for Janáček's accusation of dilettantism.) It can be said of Janáček's realism that, having begun as a stylistic tendency manifested in the use of primary speech melody, it ended by permeating the entire musical fabric, determining not only the melodic style but even the formal construction as well. At the same time, in both *Jenůfa* and *Kát'a Kabanová*, a central role is assigned to one particular motive which, on the one hand, is tangibly associated with the fundamental dramatic theme and, on the other hand, through constant recurrence and transformation, ensures the work's musical consistency from within.

The term 'monothematicism' has urged itself upon some exegetes when they have been trying to characterize the role of motivic technique in Janáček's musical dramaturgy. It is an overstatement, but a helpful and illuminating one. For there is no escaping the impression that an opera by Janáček rests on a network of motivic relationships which is steadily drawn tighter and tighter, regardless of which analytical categories one uses to explain the technical causes for the aesthetic effect. And while this web represents the structural consequences which Janáček drew from the speech inflexions of vocal melody, at the same time it also fulfils a dramaturgical function: it is able to suggest through the medium of music the inevitabilty whereby circumstances growing out of the narrowness and backwardness of village or small-town life become, in *Jenůfa* and *Kát'a Kabanová*, a tragedy of a type which is quite independent of the milieu. (Although Janáček's realism was one of the avenues of escape for a composer in the 1890s from the overwhelming presence of the Wagnerian inheritance, there can be no doubt that the idea that a steadily tightening network of motivic relationships acts as a musical metaphor for an inescapable tragic fate was Wagnerian in inspiration.)

While the derivation of instrumental melody from speech is the outcome of the deliberate attempt to create a necessary interrelationship between realistic vocal melody and orchestral structures (and Janáček's criticism of Musorgsky shows he regarded this as a matter of aesthetic and musical integrity), at the same time the actual compositional process involves an element of distancing which clearly has a bearing on Janáček's notorious objectivity towards his dramatis personae and their emotional and mental states. In contrast to Wagner, who keeps up a constant running commentary on the unfolding drama, Janáček is not present in his own person, or discoursing in his own words; he is more like an observer, standing back unnoticed behind what he has to show us, which reveals itself in its own terms. This is not the same thing as the 'impassibilité' advocated by Flaubert, for his objectivity does not conceal Janáček's sympathetic concern for Jenůfa, her foster mother, or Kát'a, especially in the great monologues which become the turning-points of the action. Nevertheless, in the immediate post-Wagnerian era, the difference between Wagner's constant asseverations of identification and involvement and Janáček's observant distancing is so pronounced that we can speak, without unwarranted fancifulness, of an inner affinity to the French and Russian realists.

The musical form which the principle of expression assumes in Janáček's operas, therefore, can be termed realist in a precise sense which defines its position in the history of ideas. It is a realism distinguished by palpable categorial factors both from the expressivity of the age of sensibility and romanticism and from the representation of affections in the baroque age. In the broad terminology historians are sometimes forced to use if they want to bring certain things to light at all, even if it means blurring some of the finer points – the alternative being eternal silence – the type of nineteenth- and twentieth-century realism represented by Janáček confronts the generalized objectivation of the baroque age and the subjective, individualistic expressivity of the age of sensibility and romanticism with an objective individualism, the historical significance and influence of which will be overlooked by those who operate only with bald 'either/or' typologies.

It is one of the commonplaces of music history that the representation of affections in baroque music is not so much a matter of giving a musical expression to the inner stirring of an emotion as of attempting to 'paint' its exterior characteristics and manifestations; another is that it was only with the onset of the age of sensibility in the latter part of the eighteenth century that a musical expressivity came into being, founded on the idea that the composer (or the interpreter, as the composer's deputy) expressed himself and laid bare the state of his own soul, or at least sought to give the aesthetic impression of doing so: in the phrase C. P. E. Bach borrowed from Horace, the artist moved others because he was himself moved.

By contrast, little attention has been paid to the clearly

defined and historically significant phenomenon that the realist principle of expression undoubtedly is. While reviving objectivation, far from sacrificing the individualization and differentiation which sensibility and romanticism gave to the musical depiction of emotions, realism actually strengthened them. What has hindered full recognition of this phenomenon is the ineradicable habit of labelling nineteenth-century music in its entirety as romantic and, to make bad worse, invariably associating romanticism with the notion of emphatically subjective emotional expression. This preconception has persisted in the general consciousness, in spite of constant corrections in matters of individual detail, and has prevented the objectivizing tendencies of the nineteenth century receiving their due. (The differences outlined here are not simply a matter of date: differences between genres also play a part; but although it is obvious that objectivation, whether baroque or realist, is manifested primarily in opera, while the subjectivation of sensibility and romanticism comes to the fore in chamber music, it does not really affect the broad distinctions between periods, because it is no accident that specific genres best represent the aesthetic trends of specific periods.) Janáček's purpose, in his tireless collecting of folk songs and speech melodies, was not to use them in the form of direct quotation – which he explicitly condemned as appropriation of the expressions of another's soul – but to learn the vocabulary and grammar of a language, in order to express himself in it, in a dramatic medium. He had a genius for observation, and one thing he shared with the Russian realists whose works he admired was that deep sympathy did not stand in the way of a relentlessly exact representation that an outsider might mistake as a sign of lack of sympathy.

But Janáček's study of speech inflexions as a means of ascertaining the expressive musical content of a language was not a purely isolated interest. That it was in line with an overriding tendency of an age which felt and described itself as being realist, is demonstrated by the case of a composer like Humperdinck. Precisely because he and Janáček were musical antipodes, Humperdinck can stand as an impeccable witness to a Zeitgeist, manifested as a common current detectable in diverse stylistic forms. Humperdinck was of that advanced breed of Wagnerian that can perhaps be called 'Bayreuthian', yet he was prepared to argue in favour of melodrama, in defiance of Wagner's strictures on the 'unsatisfyingly mixed character' of the medium. In doing so he explicitly appealed to the Zeitgeist, for he believed that melodrama was a means whereby music could satisfy the contemporary demand for realism in art.

Modern opera is moving along a road which must lead to melodrama. With the endeavour to get reality on to the stage which is endemic to our time, a form must surely be found which will answer this call of the times, and in my opinion that form is melodrama.[85]

The temper of the times was not the only connection, however, between Janáček's theory of speech melody and *fin de siècle* melodrama; they are related not only in their reflection of the same period in the history of ideas but also pragmatically, in a purely technical, musical sense, to which the undeniable difference between musical and non-musical declamation is irrelevant. In the early years of the twentieth century a reciter like Ludwig Wüllner declaimed works such as *Hexenlied* by Max von Schillings and Ernst von Wildenbruch in a manner described as 'musikalisierend': half singing, yet maintaining the intonations of speech. At the same time, however, it is striking that a style that we today would probably call 'neo-romantic' rather than realist was described by a critic like Ernst Otto Nodnagel, writing at the turn of the century in the 'modernist' era, as 'naturalistic melodrama'.[86] The discrepancy cannot be reconciled, though there is an explanation for it: it is a recurrent phenomenon that a performing style which seems the last word in realism and expressive truth when it first emerges will strike posterity as strangely stylized and mannered, and it is something the historian must make allowances for when he attempts to do justice to the image an earlier age had of itself. One is forced to the conclusion that, on the question of what realism is, we should be guided less by our own, present-day sense of reality, and more by the premises of a past which believed it was being realist even where for us the stylization is glaring.

That Janáček's theory of speech melody is realist only to the extent that it makes plausible common cause with other realist musical and musico-dramaturgical factors hardly needs to be said. Isolation of this one element is liable to lead to the terminological error (made, for example, by Pierre Boulez[87]) if bracketing together the recitative of older opera and the technique of Musorgsky's dialogue in *Marriage* and *Boris* under the one heading of realism (even if mental reservations are registered by the use of quotation marks). In other words,

Janáček's theory of speech motives is not realist in itself, strictly speaking, but only in a specific context – in so far as the term is used with specific reference to a period of art history, or at least to an important trend of such a period.

Though it may seem strange at first, one of the premisses of the musical realism manifested in Janáček's theory and practice of speech motives was nineteenth-century nationalism. Boris Asafyev recognized that realism in music, as in the other arts, is a category of reception quite as much as of production. 'When a composer selects these intonations or those from the "musical arsenal" and integrates them into his work, fixes them in the consciousness of his contemporaries, he is applying realist method.' But since every selection of 'intonations' (a term which, in Russian, embraces the diverse expressive aspects of musical form) is coloured by the composer's personality and thus is necessarily individual (a fact which Zola emphasized with regard to the novel and which therefore is essentially irrelevant to realism or naturalism), the application of realist method, the choice from the arsenal of national intonations, is by no means a guarantee that the result will be realist. 'That means that the realist method of selecting intonations does not necessarily bring with it realist music as a consequence.' It is only when the style – the chosen intonations – of an individual composer (Smetana or Janáček, Musorgsky or Tchaikovsky) is accepted and acknowledged as a national musical idiom that, in Asafyev's view, the question of the substantive realism of a musical work is ultimately decided.

By persistently underpinning the realist element in his work with the help of those everyday intonations which will convince and persuade all strata of his audience, and have without doubt become a completely real expression of ideas and emotions in the view of most people, the composer attains indisputably to realism and to general recognition of his music over the course of many generations.[88]

If musical realism and nationalism are inextricably associated in the nineteenth century, to the extent that musical 'intonations' which are always the intonations of a national language represent the criterion of a realist style, Asafyev's argument shows that this is true not only subjectively for the individual composer like Janáček, but also objectively in terms of the history of ideas. The thesis that the only way for music to achieve realism is by appropriating the musical substance of a language, and the idea that the originality of a composer must be rooted in the 'popular spirit' if it is to have any substance, are, in the nineteenth century, the age of both realism and nationalism, two sides of the same coin.

It is a long established commonplace of music history that Janáček was a realist, the paradigm, indeed, of what a musical realist should be: it seems to obviously true that it has glossed over the difficulties of pinning down precisely what is meant by it. Jan Racek, an authority on Janáček, listed the composer's theory of speech melody, his interest in folk music, and his affinity with the Russian realist novelists as sufficient evidence for his claim to the epithet.[89] Some further qualification is needed, however, when a term is habitually used as loosely as realism: in some contexts it has to do duty for nothing less than an entire aesthetic theory of the true and in others is used, or misused, as nothing more than a synonym for Tonmalerei. This has led, for example, in the case of Janáček, to the startling contradictions paraded by Michael Ewans, who at one point declares that 'Janáček's character was . . . pragmatic and realist where Wagner's was idealistic',[90] and at another says of the nature imagery in *Jenůfa* that 'these elements are "symbolic" enough to make loose talk of Janáček as a realist or naturalist absurd'[91] – as if symbolism of a poster-paint simplicity was not one of the hallmarks of the Zolaesque naturalism from which Ewans is evidently trying to dissociate Janáček and his librettists.

The first and most important consequence for Janáček's operas of his adherence to the aesthetic theory of the true was the renunciation of forms of stylization which were rooted in the traditional aesthetics of the beautiful. The grammar of the musico-dramatic speech had to abandon beautifully balanced periods, perfect syntax and prolixity, and emulate reality in 'prosaic' immediacy of expression. The rhythmic complementarity of bars and phrases, clauses and periods, which was, according to Hanslick, the primary form-building element of classic-romantic music, gave place, in the name of realism, to 'musical prose'. And Janáček's choosing, like Musorgsky in *Marriage* and *Boris*, to set prose texts is the verbal precondition, the external facet of a tendency which established its realist bona fides, in the history both of style and of ideas, by the fact that while keeping its sights on the 'prose of common life' it faced up to the central compositional issue of the period, as Wagner and Musorgsky had had to do. As the *Ring* and *Boris* both demonstrate, musical prose was a crucially important phenomenon in the historical development of music in the late nineteenth century, although it was not enough in itself to justify the epithet realist.[92]

In being pieced together from phrases of irregular and continually varying length, musical prose represented a hazardous and problematical undertaking, for although an evolutionary force was moving inexorably in that direction, it entailed nothing less than the abandonment of the periodic structure which, acting in conjunction with tonal harmony, had been the mainstay of operatic melody for the previous two centuries. Musical prose, the expression in rhythm and syntax of realism in nineteenth-century music, created a structural problem which some, like Gounod, chose to ignore and others, like Wagner, tried to solve. The possible answers, as Wagner recognized, were either leitmotivic technique or the adaptation of melody to dramatic dialogue.

Gounod was sufficiently affected by the temper of the times to experiment with setting prose – in the mid-1870s he started a *George Dandin*, after Molière, but it remained unfinished and the experiment had no definitive outcome. He avoided the formal problem by simply ignoring it, continuing to compose with quadratic periodic structures instead of allowing a musical prose to develop from the verbal prose. 'It is sometimes difficult', he wrote, 'to give prose a musical structure with any symmetry or rhythmic regularity.'[93] Symmetry is of course the central category of the aesthetics of the beautiful, and Gounod's unwillingness to forgo it is part and parcel of his explicit rejection of realism. Wholly in the spirit of French aesthetic theory of the eighteenth century, Gounod believed in art as the means for 'correcting' and restoring nature to its true, ideal self.

Let us have no more flaunting of these equivocal and noisy titles, *naturalism, realism*, and so forth! Art is Nature, yes, *in the first place*; but Nature verified, and registered, weighed – *judged*, in a word, before the tribunal of a discernment which analyses, and a reason which rectifies and restores her.[94]

If vocal melody takes the looser form of musical prose, leitmotivic technique offers a means whereby the instrumental accompaniment can act as a brace or framework, but Janáček rejected it, as his critique of Musorgsky demonstrates, because it led, in his view, to a separation of vocal and instrumental melody, which in turn created a sense of a lack of formal logic and

coherence. Janáček sought to mediate between the different
layers in the musical fabric by constructing his orchestral melody
from speech melodies too, and supplementing that by the use of
'dialogisierte Melodie', that is, by confronting the inflexions of
the people engaged in the dialogue in such a way that, even when
the audience cannot fully hear every word, the expressive musical substance of the speech creates the impression of a dialogue
in which the words of one speaker always provoke a response
from the other. (A twentieth-century successor to this has been
György Ligeti's asemantic musical dialogue.) The musical-cum-
verbal inflexions create a relationship between the characters
which renders the traditional form-building principle of rhythmic
complementarity superfluous. And it is the fact that Janáček was
able to draw form-building consequences from the speech
melodies themselves – rather than from musical structures completely alien to speech motives – which made him a composer for
whom, it can be said, realism was a stylistic principle, not merely
a condition governing his choice of subject matter, an aesthetic
viewpoint, or a source of material.

A negative consequence of Janáček's insistence on dialogue as
his dramatic medium (one thing he had in common with Wagner,
antipodal as they were in so many matters) was that he avoided
ensemble passages as much as possible, although he did not
resort to the naivety of arguing that 'everybody talking at once'
is unrealistic. The outstanding exception to that general rule is
the great ensemble in Act 3 of *Jenůfa* (comparable to the opening
of Act 3 of *Kát'a Kabanová*) and – as is the way with exceptions
to general rules – it sheds much light on the whole question of
Janáček's realism, which is by no means a simple algebraic problem to which there is a single conclusive answer. The fact that the
opera ends with a duet for Laca and Jenůfa, rather than with a
large ensemble for chorus and soloists, was no longer exceptional
in the late nineteenth century, even in Italian opera (think of
Aida). That the ensemble is a response to an event in the plot –
the discovery of the dead baby – again has precedents in
traditional dramaturgy, when some startling new development
provokes the characters assembled on the stage to opposing or
complementary reactions which are then expressed musically in
a contrapuntal ensemble, the layers in which are musically and
emotionally contrasted. Janáček, however, is not content simply
to superimpose the many divergent emotions – the horror felt by
the chorus of village people, Jenůfa's fear, the Kostelnicka's

breakdown, Laca's generosity, the magistrate's indecisiveness, Steva's pitiful embarrassment and his bride's chagrin – and elaborate all of them at length, as if each of the characters, as in the 'contemplative ensemble' of Italian opera, was sunk in his or her own feelings, regardless of anyone else. Instead, although individual phrases not infrequently interlock, they always retain the character of elements – statement, question, answer – in dialogue, but dialogue which moves so rapidly and almost incoherently that the end product is that of an ensemble, the effect of simultaneous, divergent utterance. Dialogue and ensemble are held so to speak in balance in a scene which amalgamates shocked stillness and emotional frenzy.

There is thus a dramaturgical reason for the overall effect made by this ensemble, and there is no question of the realist dialogue principle being forsaken for 'purely musical' reasons. The earlier scenes in the act, depicting the preparations for a country wedding, may superficially create the impression of picturesque light relief, but they have the precise dramatic function of delineating by musical and scenic means the milieu of the Moravian village, whose social pressures, narrowness of vision and moral rigidity form the essential preconditions for the tragic fate of which Jenůfa and the Kostelnička are the victims. (It can even be said that, as in some romantic operas, the 'local colour' becomes one of the actors, participating in the drama instead of serving merely as backdrop.) This succession of scenes culminates in the ensemble, in which the effect of 'everybody talking at once' is to make the wall of convention and gossip which hems the characters in audibly and painfully palpable.

In terms of the history of the operatic genre, a curious contrariety results from the fact that one of the premisses of the tragedy which casts its shadow over Janáček's operas is the setting in a village or small town. There appears to be a certain dichotomy in Janáček's concept of realism. On the one hand the backwardness of the provincial milieu of *Jenůfa* and *Kát'a Kabanová* is one of the conditions affecting the way the unhappy relationships between the characters resolve themselves into a drama which possesses the underlying structure of tragedy. Jenůfa, the Kostelnička and Kát'a, though 'lower class', rise musically and dramaturgically to the stylistic heights of tragedy, and the existence of tragedy in a proletarian or petty bourgeois milieu is one of the decisive criteria of realism in opera: of a realism which must be defined according to the terms of the history of the genre if it is to carry any weight. In breaking the rule of traditional stylistic class distinctions, *Jenůfa* and *Kát'a Kabanová* observe one of the principles of a realism which claimed to represent reality truly, and not as distorted by the norms of stylization: a reality in which tragedy is not the prerogative of one class.

On the other hand the setting which turns the events in the direction of tragedy is curiously free of any sense of the pressure of historical forces: this is contrary to the realist character of the work, if by realism we understand the representation of a society subject to alterations caused by concrete historical factors. By contrast to the panoramic view of a whole society depicted in the great realist novels of the nineteenth century, the social setting of Janáček's operas appears to be fixed and motionless. In fact, the unchanging rigidity of the circumstances in which Jenůfa and Kát'a stifle provides the drama with the foundation without which it would not become the tragedy that Janáček's sense of the world insisted it had to be. Realism in opera cannot simply be defined according to an unvarying list of observable features which the historian has only to enumerate like a book-keeper; rather, it constitutes a different underlying structure in the case of each composer, who selects and assembles a different combination of components according to the dictates of his specific individual view. The stylistic formula is not the result of the interpretation of the work, but the starting point.

12

The natural world
and the 'folklike tone'

The natural world in music, as in all art, is always 'second nature', using the term with the implications set out by Hegel in his *Ästhetik*. When we hear the prelude to *Das Rheingold*, the storm at the beginning of *Die Walküre* or the Forest Murmurs in *Siegfried*, it is as if nature itself speaks, at Nietzsche says, but this

quality is not due to a naivety fostered by closeness to the
elemental origins of wind or water so much as to an intellectual
capacity for reflection which conceived or conjured up the musical picture of nature as a conscious exception to the stylistic
norm: it is a cultivated, second nature which confronts culture in
a spirit of nostalgia and elegy. In summoning forth music drama
from the spirit of the symphony, Wagner laid claim to sym-
phonism as the principle behind his dramaturgy, but when he
painted these scenes of the natural world he suspended the symphonic principle of thematic-motivic working. Since Beethoven,
the law of symphonic motion has been incessant goal-
directedness, but here the law is set in abeyance while the music
expands in a stationary spread of sound, albeit animated by
interior motion. The model for this was again Beethoven: the
procedures outlined in the development section of the first movement of the Sixth Symphony and the beginning of the finale of the
same work. This expanse has in some respects neither beginning
nor end, and its start is as indeterminate as its close is unmarked.
Musical pictures of nature, in so far as the categories of beginning, middle and end are in abeyance in them, are 'formless' in a
precise sense of the word.

The discovery of a latent affinity between the simple song
which aspires to the condition of folk music and the technique
developed by Wagner for the portrayal of nature is an aesthetic
experience which cannot be avoided when the hearer encounters
Mahler's First and Third Symphonies, but it is not easy to work
out a theoretical explanation for it. The bald assertion that a folk
song, or a song 'im Volkston', as such, independent of context, is
a phenomenon of nature in music undoubtedly does not go far
enough; if anything, it requires explanation on its own account.
When, in the introduction to the first movement of the First Symphony, the 'folklike tone' of a wistful horn tune (four bars before
Figure 2) confronts material which the composer directs should
be played 'like a natural sound', there does not at first seem to be
any obvious solution to the problem of how a union which will be
satisfactory on both aesthetic and compositional, technical
grounds is to be negotiated between the melody of a strophic
song with a compact, regular periodic structure, and an amorphous and, as it were, unconfined 'natural sound' with a marked
leaning towards 'musical prose'. In fact the existence of the first
movement is triumphant proof that an answer can be found; the
explanation, however, seems to lie less with analysis of the move-

ment's structure – the observation that the development sets up
a motivic relationship between the 'song' and the 'natural sound'
and draws them jointly into the workings of the symphonic process is accurate but hardly adequate – than with aesthetics: the
musical spread in Wagner was a continuous expanse, but Mahler,
although unquestionably in Wagner's debt, designed his according to a diametrically contrary principle, namely as a discontinuous, much-fissured complex, pieced together from heterogeneous elements converging from all directions. (A collage
technique, forcing discontinuous elements together, repudiates
developmental musical processes quite as emphatically as
stationary sound does.) The result, however, was a stylistic
montage in which snatches of the song could be included without
any aesthetic incompatibility; the paradoxical thing is that, by
virtue of the fact that these quotations depart from the symphonic norm, they seem to be perfectly at home in the musical
world of the 'natural sound'. In other words, the 'song' acquires
the character of a natural phenomenon because Mahler creates a
context which allows it to appear in that light. It is entirely in
accordance with the thesis that music can assimilate the natural
world only in the form of 'second nature' that the simple appears
to be nature because of its contrast to symphonic style. What
gives the 'folklike tone' the character of reality is the act of
quotation.

The fact that Mahler set up an aesthetically precarious
relationship between song and symphony meant, therefore, not
the destruction of 'naturalness', as an uncomprehending and hostile school of criticism had it, but rather its restoration. The
folksong enthusiasts who were nettled by Mahler failed to grasp
that essentially what he had expressed in music was precisely
their own relationship to folk music; deny it though they might,
as the educated bourgeoisie – the 'Bildungsbürger' – of the
nineteenth century their reception of folk music was refracted
through the lens of 'sentimentality' (in the Schillerian sense of a
reflective capacity affected by education, culture and intellectu-
ality). The folk song was rediscovered at a time when musical
receptivity had been conditioned by the symphonic style of the
'great' music of the age, and it was this accident of timing which
led to its being accepted as a 'natural phenomenon' in music:
Mahler might be said to have transplanted these data from
'Rezeptionsgeschichte' to the history of composition.

The reflective, intellectual slant, then, was an essential constituent of the folklike tone if it was to be integrated into symphonic style: integration by means of disintegration, aesthetically, whereas technically it was achieved by motivic assimilation. In recognizing that, however, we can also see that the aesthetic incompatibility which appears to gape in the first movement of the First Symphony, between the parodic Bohemianfiddler tone ('Mit Parodie') and the quotation of the linden tree episode from *Lieder eines fahrenden Gesellen* (marked 'very simple and unpretentious, like a folk song'), is also brought to a satisfactory agreement. Both these themes, the satiric and the elegiac, are 'music about music', that is, conceived in the 'sentimental' spirit which Schiller recognized to be a factor common to both satire and elegy. And although the marking 'Mit Parodie' should be understood primarily as a performance direction, and not as the composer's aesthetic confession, it does not diminish the likelihood that, in alluding to a merriment which can turn at any moment into despair, Mahler's intention was aesthetically just as 'serious' as with the nostalgic, wistful tone he adopts in the 'linden tree' quotation. There are many passages in Mahler where it is as impossible to separate irony from sentiment as it is in Heine.

It is in penetrating beyond the level of naive identification that Mahler reveals the true complexity of the nineteenth-century relationship to folk music, and it is this that makes his quotations, or apparent quotations, speak loud and clear, after he has given them life and breath with his irony and sentiment. The exposition of that relationship is what T. W. Adorno hails as Mahler's 'realism', even 'social realism'. Mahler

> pleads musically on behalf of peasant cunning against the powers-that-be; on behalf of those who go AWOL at the prospect of marriage; on behalf of outsiders, jailbirds, starving children, losers, lost causes. Mahler is the only composer to whom the term 'social realism' could be applied, if it was not itself so depraved by power.[95]

The seditious element – the positive prejudice in favour of areas of reality and subject matter which were previously barred to music as an art: these are the realist credentials of the concerns listed by Adorno, according to the criteria which evolved during the course of the nineteenth century. The technical significance of the term is that the folklike tone, by virtue of the quotational character it assumes when placed, collage-like, in a symphonic setting, has the appearance of a phenomenon of reality which to some extent intrudes into the artificial musical structure from the world outside.

When Hans Werner Henze, on the other hand, not without political connotations, wants to make a reference to Mahler's 'realism' plausible, he emphasizes the fact that the musical language, with a vocabulary orientated in part by the 'folklike tone', is permeated by the traces of an intellectualism which attempts to get to the bottom of music, instead of naively (the Schillerian antonym of 'sentimentally') accepting tradition and its stylization.

For the first time in musical history, music is interrogating itself about the reasons for its existence and about its nature . . . Its provocation lies in its love of truth and in its consequent lack of extenuation. Like all great music, it too comes from the singing and dancing of the people; but that in no sense makes it simple, no, it makes everything real, and really difficult.[96]

The quotational character which clings so tenaciously to the folklike tone of the linden tree episode in the First Symphony is especially blatant in the posthorn episode in the Scherzo of the Third. This became the favourite target of a school of criticism which accused Mahler of triviality and inconsequentiality and proceeded to construe those alleged attributes as proof of a gulf between intention and realization. By any technical criterion the episode (third movement, Fig. 14) cannot be said to start without having been prepared for (the trumpet motive four bars before Fig. 12 is as effective a medium of mediation as the sustained string chords four bars after Fig. 13). That, however, has little or no bearing on the aesthetic effect it makes, of an abrupt and disquieting intervention 'as if from a remote distance'. The argument, initiated by Schoenberg, that the apparent triviality of many of Mahler's themes is exalted by the symphonic context into which they are integrated by motivic working and developing variation has become an established tenet in the literature about Mahler: it is high time that a defence was adopted which follows a diametrically opposite course: it is precisely by the act of forcing heterogeneous material to coexist, without glossing over the inconsistencies, that Mahler creates a panorama which truly fulfils the claim he made for the symphony: it stands as a metaphor in sound for a world which contains within itself high and low, the sophistication of fine art and artless vulgarity, with complete impartiality and with a sense of reality which is rooted in a sense of justice. In Mahler, the momentum of a deeply felt 'universalism' effortlessly overrides the most extreme incompatibilities between the multifarious contents of the one work, very much as it does in the poetry of Walt Whitman. And just as metaphysics, in the shape of transcendentalism, goes hand in hand with Whitman's heterogeneity, so in Mahler's case, in the form of the Schopenhauerian philosophy of the will, it is the inseparable accompaniment and condition of a realism which takes hold of everything without distinction, however humble, and entrusts it to the embrace of the symphony, the metaphor for a world. (Anton von Webern seems to have had something similar in mind when he said of Stravinsky's *Pribaoutki*, another work with a 'folklike tone': 'This realism leads us to the metaphysical.'[97])

That Adorno discovered realism in Mahler's folklike tone in spite of the yearning it expresses, seems surprising at first, even terminologically perverse in view of how much Mahler's conception of folk song was influenced by *Des Knaben Wunderhorn*, the *summa* of the German romantic idealization of the genre. Adorno's meaning becomes clearer, however, if we reconstruct the problems which beset the folksong craze of the eighteenth and nineteenth centuries, and review the alternative solutions with the premises on which each rested. From the time when enthusiasts begin to collect the texts, at least, of folk songs in the eighteenth century, the response to that fund of the apparently simple which turned out to be so unexpectedly complex was marked by a threefold dilemma, so to speak, originating in the uneasy relationship between the substance of the rediscovered heritage and the function it was expected to fulfil in the spiritual and intellectual lives of the educated bourgeoisie.

First of all, the collectors' decision to be selective, to separate the gold from the dross as Herder put it, was both inevitable and dangerous. It was inevitable because the image of the folk cherished by the middle-class collectors had less to do with the reality of the labouring classes than with a nostalgic but Utopian and phantasmal ideal. The consequence was the transfiguration of the folk song, and this was the source of the danger: the historical existence of folk culture was already put at risk by the onset of the industrial revolution, and being rediscovered 'from above' brought it to a complete standstill. Idealization of folk culture created a desire to restore it, but restoration meant petrifaction.

Secondly, there seemed to be no answer to the question as to whether or not it was permissible to modify folk songs, as they always had been modified. It was a condition of their existence that they were constantly subject to change as a matter of performance practice, and it was contrary to their nature if one form of a song was netted as fixed and definitive, mounted as a 'monument of musical art' and made an object of philological study. 'Folk songs', wrote Wilhelm Heinrich Riehl in 1848, 'are not once-and-for-all finished things, but are in a constant state of becoming . . . Our ancient folk melodies are not dead "reliques", history lives and breathes in them.' On the other hand it was doubtful whether the educated bourgeois who had gone out on the hunt for folk songs actually possessed the qualifications to make a legitimate contribution to the traditional process of folk song, and to modify texts or tunes in a way that prolonged their lives. The purist philologists like Jacob Grimm and Ludwig Erk in the one camp, and the poets like Arnim and Brentano – the compilers of *Des Knaben Wunderhorn* – and Zuccalmaglio in the other, who modified and added to the traditional material they collected and thereby made it something of their own, both had some claim to be in the right on the matter.

Thirdly, once appropriated by the educated bourgeoisie, the folk song was inevitably placed in a musical context dominated by classic-romantic art music. That context as such could not be banished from the aesthetic consciousness, and virtually the only way the folk song could be integrated into it was by being interpreted and treated according to the postulate of a 'rhetoric of tones': the 'folklike tone' becomes a form of colouration or characterization available for musicians to adopt at need, like the tones of elegy, ballad or hymn. But in the case of the folklike tone, that role was at odds with the principle that in adopting it a composer must speak from the depths of his own national consciousness or commit the crime of aesthetic 'inauthenticity'. There was thus an awkward contradiction between the optional nature of the tone (which was a condition of its aesthetic integration in the context of the art music of the eighteenth and nineteenth centuries) and its claim to represent the 'spirit of the people' (which was the premiss of the tone's authenticity). (Did Glinka cease to be 'authentic' when he adopted the Spanish tone instead of the Russian?)

There is virtually no possibility of a definitive resolution of these problems, and a 'realist' approach to them – that is,

measuring up to the contradictions and the historical situation –
would also appear to be almost impossible. It is not, in fact,
immediately obvious that realist is the right epithet for the course
Mahler adopted, but a plausible case can be made for its use if the
characteristics of his folklike tone are studied in the entire context rather than in isolation. While he did not resort to explanation or self-justification, his working philosophy is revealed in
the overt sympathy for an all-inclusive conception of folk song,
one that does not apply principles of selection which reduce the
tradition as they transfigure it; in the complete disregard of
philology in his uninhibited adaptation of folk material to suit
himself, following in the footsteps of Arnim and Brentano in that
respect, though he was completely unaware of it; and finally in
the tendency not so much to repudiate the eighteenth- and
nineteenth-century 'rhetoric of tones' as to take it to a radical
extreme.

The philological approach to folk song, advocated by Jacob
Grimm and practised by Ludwig Erk, can be called 'positivist',
without any disparagement being intended. There is undoubtedly some justification, at least, for the thesis that what has been
handed down from the past should be left inviolate. But it is not
'realist' because it completely overlooks the crucial condition of
the folk song's existence, the continual process of change and
modification, affecting text and music alike. On the other hand
the kind of emendation of traditional material practised on a
generous scale by Arnim and Brentano – with Goethe's
approval, be it said – ran the risk of 'romanticization' when, as
happened most notoriously in the case of Zuccalmaglio, the
underlying principle was used to justify an 'idealization' of folk
song, which meant bringing it into line with bourgeois expectations by means not of selection alone but also of restoration and
refurbishment.

The virtue of philological 'positivism' was that the whole tradition was accepted – but only at the price of petrifaction; the
virtue of 'romanticization' was that it recognized modification
and amendment as the life-blood of a folk art-form – but the
price, in practice, was embourgeoisement: either way lay alienation. Mahler's 'realism' avoids both by accepting the full extent
of tradition without regard to bourgeois norms at the same time
as it attempts to involve itself in the continuing life of the folk
song by emending and modifying. And Mahler's licence to do
this came not from any pretence of closeness to the sources of folk

song – a pretence the nineteenth-century positivists rightly recognized to be an illusion – but, quite the reverse, from the consciousness of an unbridgeable historical distance. That distance is what is, so to speak, 'composed out' when Mahler incorporates a folk song into a symphony: the posthorn tune, sounding 'as if from a remote distance' in the Scherzo of the Third Symphony, can be taken as the archetypal example of Mahler's appropriation of the 'folklike tone', and the acoustic distance is symbolic of the historical distance which, far from denying, he deliberately emphasizes. The authenticity of the folklike tone is not owed to any illusory identification but to a nostalgia which is unmistakably real. And 'realism' does not consist in the naivety with which some composers write movements 'in the style of a folk song' – as if the diatonicism of *Die Meistersinger*, which owes everything to the prior existence of the chromaticism of *Tristan*, had never existed (Mahler knew better, as the Seventh Symphony shows). It consists in the 'sentimental' (elegiac or satirical) tone Mahler adopted in order to push home the point that, paradoxically, it is as something lost, and given up for lost, that folk song is not lost.

13

The dialectics of the concept of reality

It is virtually inconceivable that a concept of realism which will serve the purposes of the history of art can be formulated without a certain measure of philosophical disingenuousness, whether involuntary or assumed. While a reach-me-down equation of reality with what can be found in a daily newspaper would undoubtedly impose self-defeating limitations, on the other hand no good purpose would be served if, having set out to survey the characteristics of realism in nineteenth-century art, one lost one's way in the dialectics of a philosophical enquiry which ended by reducing the concept of reality to a labyrinth of problems as fascinating as they are insoluble. (The charge of a certain wilfulness in ignoring the principle of 'continuous reflection', which in essence forces a thinker to question all categories incessantly and simultaneously, is one the historian must admit to if he shuns the step of changing his calling for that of philosophy.)

But if there is some justification for the decision to refrain from constantly passing from pragmatics to theory and thence to metatheory, it is still not entirely a waste of effort to mention, in broad outline at least, some of the musico-aesthetic consequences which would result from an attempt to pursue the ramifications of the concept of reality for any distance. Ever since the aesthetics of the beautiful was displaced by the aesthetics of the true, the problem of what 'true' reality 'really' is has plagued compositional practice, as well as theories about music.

The elementary convention that only what is intersubjectively observable is real arouses some immediately obvious objections, but in the nineteenth century it formed the main premiss in support of a realism which from around 1850 onward was propounded as the 'order of the day' in art and art theory. But the simple maxim which served the publicists well for decades, during which it became firmly established in the public consciousness, was exposed in the end to the probings of a theory of knowledge which aesthetic theory, even when put into practice and documented in works of art, could not ignore indefinitely. The naive concept of reality was gradually displaced by a scepticism which spread from the philosophers to infect the public in general. And without going into the profound changes which affected epistemology from Kant to Ernst Mach in any detail, we can make a start with the fundamental thesis that, by philosophical criteria, reality is not a straightforward, direct *donnée*, but is constituted as a relationship between the amorphous material received by the senses, and the categorial form contributed by the perceiving consciousness. In other words, understanding of what things are on their own terms is simultaneously made possible and distorted by the creation of categorial forms to accommodate the impressions we receive of those things: comprehending and constructing are two aspects of the same process.

In the circumstances, either the formative factor or the distorting factor in the activity of the consciousness can be emphasized. Like Kant, we can focus on the contribution the categorial apparatus makes to the constitution of reality; or else, like Mach, distrusting the 'additives' contributed by the consciousness as it 'structures' what is perceived, we can look for 'true reality' in the material received by the senses in its amorphous state: the material must be teased away from the categorial structure bit by bit – although it is impossible for it ever to be entirely free of it. 'True' realism would by that criterion be impressionism, represented in music by Oscar Bie in aesthetic theory and – by general consensus – Claude Debussy in compositional practice.

It is unnecessary to itemize the reasons why Debussy's style is commonly compared to the contemporary – or slightly earlier – style of impressionism in painting, because the crucial factor is obviously a mode of thought of a relatively high degree of abstraction. At any event, the fact that the subjects Debussy liked to depict in his piano music betray a marked preference for the fluid and the indefinite (*Jardins sous la pluie, Reflets dans l'eau, Voiles*) rather than for the clear-cut and well-defined is less significant than a condition, common to Debussy's music as a whole, of stasis animated only internally. Hans Mersmann interpreted this characteristic as an expression of 'passivity': unlike the tradition of Beethoven and – especially – Wagner, whose processes he denounced, Debussy's music is not goal-directed, but seems to circle within itself, and to cease rather than close.

The technical features – the dissolution of functional harmony, the disruption of regular, tonally based periodic structure and the cessation of the thematic-motivic working which Debussy felt to be pedantic but which had formed the 'teleological' element in music in the nineteenth century, in conjunction with tonal harmony – may amount to the abrogation of the traditional categorial apparatus pertaining to musical structure, or at the very least to undermining it by the act of 'composing out' the doubts Debussy had of it; but, unless one succumbs to the siren song of Giestesgeschichte, it is clear that direct and unqualified parallels or analogies should not be drawn between those features and the scepticism which led to nineteenth-century realism, in its closing phase, assuming the form of impressionism. At the same time, there is no mistaking an inner affinity which is not the product merely of wishful thinking.

The claim that a general distrust of all categorial systems – that is, a particular kind of reaction to the epistemological problems which came, as described above, to beset the concept of reality – was the decisive link between compositional practice and modes of philosophical thought at the end of the nineteenth century may appear at first blush a highly abstract hypothesis with little likelihood of being borne out by the analytical evidence of hard facts. Yet it can be substantiated to an extent that should satisfy pragmatically inclined historians.

It is possible at all events to reconstruct what a contemporary writer like Oscar Bie meant by the expression 'musical impressionism'. Under the influence of the physicist–philosopher Ernst Mach the theory had developed that traditional structures and systems were no more than mental concepts and that phenomena were essentially isolated and momentary experiences; the dismissal of structures enabled Bie to draw the conclusion that isolated sound phenomena alone represented the 'true reality' of music. The conviction that only when they were isolated and removed from any context were things wholly themselves and 'truly real' was the main premiss supporting an impressionism which was thus seen to be a variant – to some extent a 'more philosophical' one – of realism.

The recognition that categorial systems are not inherent in the nature of things but are constructs of the perceptive consciousness had a considerable influence on thought in general in the twentieth century. In the art of the period, including the 'new music', it led to the adoption of some radically different positions: from Ernst Křenek's postulate of a boundless freedom to invent musical axioms to John Cage's demolition of all relationships and sense-associations between sounds. A genuine mystic, Cage believes that is the path which leads to the true nature of music – or, more precisely, of sound. But while they represent probably the most extreme views, both positions unmistakably derive from the epistemological issues surrounding the concept of reality: compositional practice, and above all experimental composition, is affected by the dialectics of concepts of reality in a very practical and palpable sense.

The emergence of impressionism out of realism was thus a less contradictory process than it might appear to be, and much the same is true of the development of late-nineteenth-century naturalism into expressionism. The school of music history which lists characteristics instead of reconstructing issues would call the succeeding of the one by the other a change of direction, but the relationship between them is rather more complicated than that, and regulated by what Hegel called 'specific negation'.

The most extreme document of musical expressionism is Arnold Schoenberg's monodrama *Erwartung*. That it exemplifies a type of drama inspired by Strindberg, whose adherents Schoenberg and his circle expressly acknowledged themselves to be, is obvious and has never been disputed; and this literary premiss had a profound influence on the music. The full process of transition from naturalism to expressionism took place within the compass of Strindberg's oeuvre, with a positively programmatic rigour. In *The Father*, for example, the dichotomy between the naturalistic 'view from without', which makes the protagonist the object of merciless observation, and the expressionistic 'view from within', whereby the other characters become projections of the central character's state of mind, forms the essential theme of the play and determines its dramatic structure – to the discomfiture of directors.

The fact that the stylistic transition is plain to see in a work like *The Father* does not mean, however, that it is as easily explicable in terms of the history of ideas. And a similar ambivalence in the musical 'modernism' of around 1900 is at first almost impossible to explain, although the data are clear enough in themselves, because the power of observation is distorted by preconceptions which derive from over-reliance on terminological distinctions.

At the time of writing *Elektra*, Richard Strauss was the leading exponent of modernism; it is surely, however, the most advanced work he ever ventured on. In general terms, the difference between naturalistic Tonmalerei and expressionistic psychography is detectable in it but is by no means as stark as might be expected by anyone who believes abstract stylistic formulas hold the key to such matters. Strauss provides Tonmalerei of the utmost vividness for the procession of beasts brought to the palace for sacrifice: the shuffling and lurching of the animals, the muffled curses of the drovers, the swish of a whip (Figs 127–30). A short time later comes Clytemnestra's brooding on the horror that overtakes her in the small hours (Fig. 186: 'Und doch kriecht zwischen Tag und Nacht . . . ') to an orchestral accompaniment which, while it owes something still to Wagner's *Ring*, momentarily admits to its chronological proximity and inner affinity to Schoenberg's *Erwartung*. The bleak sonorities of Clytemnestra's scene, expressing the most profound terrors with all the more horror because they remain intangible, adumbrate a musical expressionism, the stylistic implications of which Strauss then rejected. At more or less the same time that Schoenberg's exploration of expressionist style and technique was opening the path that led from 'modernism' to the 'new music', Strauss found himself unable to face the stylistic consequences that his unquestionable technical facility would have allowed him to draw.

A musical modernism in which naturalism and expressionism lie cheek by jowl (another example is Franz Schreker's *Der ferne Klang*) causes a strange fog to descend on the familiar aesthetic categories in the music historian's arsenal of stereotyped concepts. In terms of the history of ideas, too, the general pattern that emerges is very confusing.

The historical fact that expressionism – at least in literature – sprang from naturalism rather than from (neo-) romanticism is bound to seem paradoxical and scarcely comprehensible if the word 'naturalism' triggers the thought of Tonmalerei first and foremost. A music historian who takes it as read that an 'expressive principle' was the driving force behind both romanticism and expressionism is likely to react by reflecting that the historical evolution of music is simply not analogous to that of literature; although such a thought might not be tenable in terms of the history of ideas, it has an obvious attraction when one's own discipline seems to be under attack. But it has already been observed that in Strindberg naturalism and expressionism complement rather than contradict each other; and the relationship becomes fully comprehensible if one recognizes that romantic expressiveness and expressionistic expressiveness – for all that a historical link exists between them in Wagner – are two fundamentally different things. The idea of an 'expressive principle', uniting heterogeneous entities and implying a continuity which did not in fact exist, misleads by its crude and superficial oversimplification.

In spite of various comments by Schoenberg, which are open to misinterpretation, it is not the artist's subjective self which presses for expression in either literary or musical expresionism. The psychological outburst registered in works such as *Erwartung*, or the Piano Piece opus 11 no. 3, occurs without personal contribution in a sense – even when it is his own individual feelings or consciousness that the artist seeks to set down in words or music. Never for a moment does the artist abandon the position of an observer and recorder of what emerges from himself: that is as true of expressionism as it is of naturalism. Thus, in spite of the expressive forces it unleashes, expressionism, unlike romanticism or neo-romanticism, is not really a 'subjective' style serving to exteriorize and objectivize what Hegel called 'subjective inwardness'. The subjective self has contracted to an observer who fastens hold of the psychic phenomena which come to light, whether they originate in himself or in others. Expressionist expressiveness is therefore, broadly speaking, 'alienated', in the psychoanalytical sense. At the turn of the century the spirit of the age was a positivist and scientific one (as psychoanalysis itself bears witness), and that spirit was what allowed expressionism to emerge from naturalism. Richard Strauss, even as 'expressionist', was nearer to Flaubert's 'impassibilité' than to Schumann's 'Innigkeit'.

14

Conclusion

Realism, manifested in individual works by Berlioz, Verdi and Bizet, Musorgsky, Janáček and Mascagni, Strauss and Mahler, was never the dominant style in music at any point in the nineteenth century. Music kept the flag of romanticism flying in a generally positivist age, with neo-romanticism rising to continue the trend before the end of the century was reached; the fact that a phenomenon which can be called musical realism existed simultaneously alongside the predominant romanticism, at times sharing some of its characteristics, and that moreover it was fully recognized as such by contemporaries, is not in itself enough to qualify, to any significant extent, the anomaly – a remarkable one from the point of view of the philosophy of history – that existed between music on the one hand and contemporary literature and painting on the other.

To speak of a realist tendency, as one component in the heterogeneous style of an age which was divided between romanticism and realism, would be inappropriate and misleading. For although the observable phenomena which can be designated realist are interrelated, they do not form a well-defined nexus characterizing a particular group of works which could then – if that *was* the case – be seen to represent 'officially' the realism of nineteenth-century music. Methodologically, if we are to abstract a result from the analyses of the individual instances, it is rather the case that they form a theoretical model which serves the function of an 'ideal type' as defined by Max Weber.

An 'ideal type', briefly, is a hypothetical construction in which a historian assembles a number of phenomena which in historical reality are observed haphazardly and always in different combinations, and relates and compares them to each other in order to bring out the connection between them. It is then possible, in circumstances where only some of the phenomena are encountered together, and perhaps in combination with yet other elements, to discern the significative structure which allows the single detail to be understood and interpreted through the functional nexus of which it forms part.

The characteristics of musical realism in the nineteenth century – some peculiar to that period, some actually of earlier origin – include aesthetic premisses such as the accentuation of the true instead of the beautiful as the goal of art and the element of sedition and rebellion implied by the choice of subject matter once regarded as unsuitable; dramaturgical trends such as the abandonment of the rule of stylistic class distinctions and the concern to lay solid historical and social factual foundations for operatic plots; and finally compositional phenomena such as the dissolution of periodic structure in musical prose, 'dialogisierte Melodie', the attempt to reproduce speech intonations, and the enlarged scope of Tonmalerei and the depiction of emotion with the decline of stylization. Any expectation, however, that all these characteristics are to be found assembled in certain works, which would then be unquestionably realist, is disappointed and refuted by historical fact, just as theories which add up with arithmetical neatness are generally useless in the writing of history. Nevertheless, it can be shown that there is a significative and functional association between all these characteristics which justifies the hypothesis of the ideal type; and the fact that an inner connection can be constructed provides a foundation for the thesis that for methodological purposes nineteenth-century musical realism represents a theoretical model which can serve as a starting point both in the analysis of individual works and in the attempt to reveal the associations between works which outwardly – stylistically – appear to have virtually nothing in common.

There is an immediately obvious, close connection between the loss of constraint in the representation of emotion – as an act of rebellion against stylization – and the trend towards musical prose in the form of irregular phrase structures according to the demands of the text and the dramatic moment, even though that general statement at once requires qualification in the particular cases of the two leading musical dramatists of the period. Verdi, characteristically, strove for realism in the representation of emotion without accepting the dissolution of traditional periodic structure as an inevitable consequence. On the other hand, in the case of all Wagner's music dramas from *Das Rheingold* onwards, the musical prose and an expressivity of unprecedented vigour and effectiveness are combined with a dramatic structure in which, as productions in recent years have emphasized, an Ibsenite, even Strindbergian realism lurks behind the romantic spirit of its mythological ambience, but that does not mean that the historian, without further ado, can equate the mythology with the realist trend of the age, in terms of the history of ideas. When an ideal type is constructed incorporating the various realist phenomena, the plausibility of the association thus revealed serves to assist recognition of how the non-realist features in Verdi and Wagner, the phenomena which cannot be included in the ideal type, depart from the general pattern and require explanation in terms of the particular historical circumstances: Verdi's sense that musical prose was incompatible with the essence of the popularity of Italian opera; Wagner's inner dependence on the romantic inheritance, which influenced not only his choice of subject matter but also his compositional technique, in that the mythological structure is vital to the development of Leitmotiv.

It would undoubtedly be illuminating if a composer applied the compositional techniques of musical prose, 'dialogisierte Melodie' and the sacrifices of stylization to expressivity in operas with subjects taken from the present time or the immediate past, set in a 'low-class' milieu and yet aspiring to the dignity of tragedy, and finally giving at least a rudimentary impression of the historical and social mechanisms which affect the fate of individuals. In a drama of bourgeois or proletarian life, prose – musical or verbal – is an appropriate metaphor for the prose of their everyday lives; conversely the third estate has as much right to intense emotions, rising above everyday 'prosaic' levels, and to a tragic mode of expression for those emotions as the aristocracy, which justifies the heightened emotional expressiveness without which opera – by contrast to the repression of emotional expression in the realist spoken play of the nineteenth century – can hardly exist.

The fact remains that *Carmen* and *Cavalleria rusticana* eschew musical prose because Bizet and Mascagni did not wish to take risks with the well-tried formulas of operatic popularity (and perhaps, too, because they discerned, or suspected, the dramaturgical association between leitmotivic technique, the formal backbone of Wagner's musical prose, and the mythological subject matter). This is at odds with a concept of realism which aspires to nothing more than simple stylistic description – in terms of enumerating the recurrence of certain characteristics in various works – but it is not sufficient reason for speaking either of an aesthetic shortcoming in Italian verismo (a stylistic inconsequence) or – vice versa – of a methodological inadequacy of the proposed theoretical model. An ideal type is neither a norm, from which aesthetic judgements may be derived, nor a given, historically observable set of facts; it is a hypothetical construction compiled by the historian, to which constellations of facts found in musical reality can be compared and related, with the purpose of enabling their interpretation as components of significative or functional nexuses.

The claim can therefore be made that behind all the divergent tendencies and stylistic divisions of the late nineteenth century an underlying pattern is discernible which makes it possible to relate to one another phenomena which historically have nothing in common, being associated with such contrasted entities as mythological music drama and veristic opera. A latent musicohistorical connection thus comes to light between works – *Der Ring des Nibelungen*, *Carmen*, *Boris Godunov* – which were written at roughly the same time but possess marked stylistic differences: a connection, be it said, which consists less in the recurrence of a certain constellation of characteristics than in a theoretical model which survives as a structure common to them all even when the separate components are present only selectively; by making the recognition of that connection possible, the concept of musical realism fulfils a valuable historiographical function and as such it will be indispensable for as long as historians of music do not despair in their pursuit of the goal of elucidating the inner unity of an epoch.

References

1 Hans Albrecht, 'Impressionismus', *Musik in Geschichte und Gegenwart*, VI (Kassel, 1957), coll. 1053–4.

2 Vladimir Karbusicky, *Empirische Musiksoziologie* (Wiesbaden, 1975), 233–51.

3 Albrecht Riethmüller, *Die Musik als Abbild der Realität* (Wiesbaden, 1976), 18.

4 Theodor W. Adorno, *Einleitung in die Musiksoziologie* (Frankfurt am Main, 1962), 216.

5 Ferruccio Busoni, *Entwurf einer neuen Ästhetik der Tonkunst* (Frankfurt am Main, 1974), 23.

6 Arnold Schoenberg, *Style and Idea*, 2nd edn (London, 1975), 450.

7 Kurt Weill, *Ausgewählte Schriften* (Frankfurt am Main, 1975), 55.

8 Norman Cazden, 'Towards a theory of realism in music', *Journal of aesthetics and art criticism*, 10 (1951), 150.

9 Philipp Spitta, *Zur Musik* (Berlin, 1892), 398.

10 Gustave Planche, 'Moralité de la poésie', *Revue des deux mondes*, 4ᵉ série, 1 (1835), 259.

11 Friedrich Chrysander, 'Händels Instrumentalkompositionen für grosses Orchester', *Vierteljahresschrift für Musikwissenschaft*, 3 (1887), 178.

12 Hermann Hettner, 'Die romantische Schule', in *Schriften zur Literatur* (Berlin, 1959), 66; F. T. Vischer in the preface to the Stuttgart 1861 edn of *Kritische Gänge*, II.

13 Michel Butor, *Essays zur modernen Literatur und Musik* (Munich, 1965), 66.

14 Franz Brendel, *Geschichte der Musik in Italien, Deutschland und Frankreich*, 4th edn (Leipzig, 1867), 564.

15 Friedrich Schlegel, *Über das Studium der griechischen Poesie* (1797) (Bad Godesberg, 1947), 58; 75.

16 Karl Köstlin, in Friedrich Theodor Vischer, *Ästhetik oder Wissenschaft des Schönen* (1857) (Munich, 1923), V, 242–3.

17 Brendel, *Geschichte der Musik*, 552.

18 Friedrich Schlegel, *Gesamtausgabe* (Munich, 1967), II, 208.

19 *Ibid.*, II, 254.

20 Vischer, *Ästhetik*, V, 242.

21 G. W. F. Hegel, *Ästhetik*, ed. F. Bassenge (Frankfurt am Main, n.d.), II, 317.
22 *Ibid.*, 316.
23 *Ibid.*
24 *Ibid.*, I, 161.
25 Hermann von Waltershausen, *Der Freischütz* (Munich, 1920), 70.
26 *Ibid.*, 71.
27 *Ibid.*, 73.
28 *Ibid.*, 77.
29 L. Tieck, 'Symphonien', *Phantasien über die Kunst, für Freunde der Kunst*, in Wilhelm Heinrich Wackenroder, *Werke und Briefe* (Heidelberg, 1967), 255.
30 Carl Seidel, *Charinomos* (Magdeburg, 1828), 10.
31 Rudolf Louis, *Deutsche Musik der Gegenwart* (Munich, 1912), 105.
32 Romain Rolland, *Musiciens d'aujourd'hui* (Paris, 1908), 124.
33 Hermann Kretzschmar, *Führer durch den Konzertsaal* (Leipzig, 1891), I, 179–80.
34 Theodor W. Adorno, *Klangfiguren* (Frankfurt am Main, 1959), 192.
35 Christian Hermann Weisse, *System der Ästhetik als Wissenschaft von der Idee der Schönheit*, new edn (Hildesheim, 1966), I, 182.
36 Richard Wagner, *Oper und Drama. Sämtliche Schriften und Dichtungen* (Leipzig, n.d.), III, 283.
37 Hermann Lotze, *Geschichte der Ästhetik in Deutschland* (Munich, 1868), 339.
38 Peter Rummenhöller, *Einführung in die Musiksoziologie* (Wilhelmshaven, 1978), 179.
39 *Ibid.*, 184.
40 Georg Knepler, *Musikgeschichte des 19. Jahrhunderts* (Berlin, 1961), II, 830.
41 *Ibid.*, I, 516.
42 Fritz Martini, 'Das Problem des Realismus im 19. Jahrhundert und die Dichtung Wilhelm Raabes', *Dichtung und Volkstum*, 36 (1935), 271.
43 Ernst Bücken, 'Romantik und Realismus', *Festschrift Arnold Schering* (Berlin, 1937), 46.
44 Ernst Bücken, *Die Musik des 19. Jahrhunderts bis zur Moderne* (Wildpark-Potsdam, 1929), 183.
45 Quoted in Bücken, 'Romantik und Realismus', 47.
46 Wolfgang Gertler, *Robert Schumann in seinen frühen Klavierwerken* (Leipzig, 1931), 42.
47 *Ibid.*, 43.
48 *Ibid.*, 14; 45.
49 *Ibid.*, 27.
50 Louise Otto, 'Die Nibelungen als Oper', *Neue Zeitschrift für Musik*, 23 (1845), 50.

51 Ernst Lichtenhahn, 'Musikalisches Biedermeier und Vormärz', *Schweizer Beiträge zur Musikwissenschaft*, 4 (1980), 7.
52 Hermann Abert, W. A. *Mozart* (Leipzig, 1923), I, 420.
53 *Ibid.*, I, 431.
54 *Ibid.*, I, 667.
55 Hans Költzsch, *Franz Schubert in seinen Klaviersonaten* (Leipzig, 1927), 55.
56 Théophile Gautier, in *La Presse*, February 1851.
57 Eduard Krüger, *System der Tonkunst* (Leipzig, 1866), 235–6.
58 Bücken, *Die Musik des 19. Jahrhunderts*, 183–4; 273.
59 Guido Adler, *Handbuch der Musikgeschichte*, 2nd edn (Berlin, 1930), 963.
60 Paul Henry Lang, *Music in Western Civilization* (London, 1942), 846.
61 Oscar Bie, *Die moderne Musik und Richard Strauss* (Berlin, 1906), 16.
62 Theodor W. Adorno, in *Die Musik*, 26/9 (June 1934), 712.
63 A. B. Marx, *Die Musik des neunzehnten Jahrhunderts und ihre Pflege: Methode der Musik*, 3rd edn (Leipzig, 1873), 118–19.
64 Bie, *Die moderne Musik und Richard Strauss*, 28.
65 To Giulio Ricordi, 20 November 1880, in *Letters of Giuseppe Verdi*, sel., transl. and ed. by Charles Osborne (London, 1971), 212–13.
66 Dieter Schnebel, 'Die schwierige Wahrheit des Lebens: Zu Verdis musikalischem Realismus', *Musik-Konzepte 10: Giuseppe Verdi* (Munich, 1979), 66.
67 Qvamme Borre, 'Verdi e il realismo', *Atti del terzo congresso internazionale de studi Verdiani, Milano 1972* (Parma, 1974), 408.
68 David Kimbell, *Verdi in the age of Italian romanticism* (Cambridge, 1981), 642 (chapter: 'Verdi and "realism": La traviata').
69 Walter Niemann, *Die Musik seit Richard Wagner* (Berlin and Leipzig, 1913), 94; 97.
70 Egon Voss, 'Verismo in der Oper', *Die Musikforschung*, 31 (1978), 303.
71 *The Musorgsky Reader. A life of Modeste Petrovich Musorgsky in letters and documents*, ed. and transl. by Jay Leyda and Sergei Bertensson (New York, 1970), 111–12.
72 Victor Seroff, *Das mächtige Häuflein* (Zurich, 1963), 102.
73 *The Musorgsky Reader*, 203.
74 Jacques Handschin, *Mussorgski* (Zurich, 1924), 14–15.
75 Oskar von Riesemann, *Modest Petrowitsch Mussorgsky* (Munich, 1926), 121–38; Michel-Dimitri Calvocoressi, *Modest Mussorgsky* (London, 1956), 81–95.
76 Richard Taruskin, 'Realism as preached and practiced: the Russian Opéra Dialogué', *Musical Quarterly*, 56 (1970), 431–54.
77 Igor Stravinsky and Robert Craft, *Conversations with Igor Stravinsky* (London, 1979), 44.

78 Viktor Šklovskij, *Theorie der Prosa* (Frankfurt am Main, 1966), 15.
79 Georges Bizet, *Lettres à un ami* (Paris, 1909).
80 Paul Bekker, *Musikgeschichte als Geschichte der musikalischen Formwandlungen* (Berlin and Leipzig, 1926), 207–8.
81 Donald Jay Grout, *A History of Western Music* (New York, 1960), 549.
82 Niemann, *Die Musik seit Richard Wagner*, 91.
83 Alfred Bruneau, *La musique française* (Paris, 1901).
84 Arthur Seidl, *Neuzeitliche Tondichter und zeitgenössische Tonkünstler* (Regensburg, 1926), I, 61–2.
85 Letter of 2 November 1898, quoted by Wolfram Humperdinck in *Engelbert Humperdinck* (Frankfurt am Main, 1965), 238–9.
86 Ernst Otto Nodnagel, *Jenseits von Wagner und Liszt* (Königsberg, 1902), 155.
87 Pierre Boulez, *Anhaltspunkte* (Stuttgart, 1972), 23–5.
88 Boris Assafjew, *Die musikalische Form als Prozess* (Berlin, 1976), 292.
89 Jan Racek, *Leoš Janáček*, 2nd edn (Leipzig, 1971), 88.
90 Michael Ewans, *Janáček's tragic operas* (London, 1977), 14.
91 *Ibid.*, 31.
92 Hermann Danuser, *Musikalische Prosa* (Regensburg, 1975).
93 In a letter to Mrs Weldon, quoted by Gerald Abraham in *Slavonic and Romantic Music* (London, 1968), 85.
94 Charles Gounod, *Autobiographical reminiscences* [transl.] by W. Hely Hutchinson (London, 1896), 248.
95 T. W. Adorno, *Mahler: eine musikalische Physiognomik* (Frankfurt am Main, 1960), 67.
96 Hans Werner Henze, *Music and politics: Collected writings 1952–81*, transl. by Peter Labanyi (London, 1982), 157–8.
97 Quoted by H. H. Stuckenschmidt in *Arnold Schoenberg*, transl. by Humphrey Searle (London, 1977), 260.

Index

Abert, Hermann, 52, 55
Adler, Guido, 56
Adorno, Theodor Wiesengrund, 8–9, 39, 58, 109, 111
Albrecht, Hans, 1–2
Aristotle, 9, 17–18, 21
Arnim, Achim von, 111–13
Asafyev, Boris, 101
Auerbach, Erich, 61, 80
Austen, Jane, 57

Bach, Carl Philipp Emanuel, 22, 27, 98
Bach, Johann Sebastian, 14, 48, 51
Balakirev, Mily, 72, 73
Balzac, Honoré de, 81
Beethoven, Ludwig van, 8–9, 21–2, 26, 31, 37, 38–40, 79, 107, 116
Bekker, Paul, 87–8
Benjamin, Walter, 24, 73
Berlioz, Hector, 2, 29–31, 34, 35, 36, 38–43, 56, 120
Bie, Oscar, 57–8, 62, 68, 116–17
Bizet, Georges, 13, 71, 76, 87–94, 120, 123
Boulez, Pierre, 100
Brahms, Johannes, 12, 14, 15, 76
Brecht, Bertolt, 6–7, 78
Brendel, Franz, 29–31, 34
Brentano, Clemens von, 111–13
Bruckner, Anton, 14
Bruneau, Alfred, 71, 92
Bücken, Ernst, 46, 49, 51, 56
Busoni, Ferruccio, 10–11
Butor, Michel, 28–9
Byron, George Gordon, Lord, 39–42

Cage, John, 117
Cazden, Norman, 13
Champfleury, Jules, 30, 53, 60, 87
Charpentier, Gustave, 76, 93–4
Chernïshevsky, Nikolai, 73
Chrysander, Friedrich, 15–16

Cornelius, Peter, 82
Courbet, Gustave, 40, 53–4, 89
Curtius, Ernst Robert, 20

Dargomïzhsky, Alexander, 73–4
Debussy, Claude, 72, 116
Diderot, Denis, 15
Dumas, Alexandre, *fils*, 65

Eisler, Hanns, 6–7
Engels, Friedrich, 4
Erk, Ludwig, 112–13
Ewans, Michael, 102

Felsenstein, Walter, 89–91
Ficker, Rudolf von, 43
Fink, Gottfried Wilhelm, 40–1
Flaubert, Gustave, 5, 27, 60, 64, 92, 120
Freud, Sigmund, 57

Galilei, Vincenzo, 22–3
Gautier, Théophile, 53–4, 89
Gertler, Wolfgang, 47–8, 51
Giordano, Umberto, 62
Glinka, Mikhail, 112
Goebbels, Joseph, 58
Goethe, Johann Wolfgang von, 16, 30, 113
Gogol, Nikolai, 72–3, 77, 78
Goncourt, Edmond & Jules de, 5, 89, 93
Gounod, Charles, 103
Grillparzer, Franz, 35
Grimm, Jacob, 112–13
Grout, Donald Jay, 88

Handel, George Frideric, 15
Hanslick, Eduard, 3, 21, 102
Haydn, Joseph, 45
Hegel, Georg Wilhelm Friedrich, 8, 19, 30, 33–5, 56, 106, 117, 119–20

129

130　　　　　　　　　*Index*